Power

Nick Dear's plays include *The Villains' Opera* (RNT, 1993); *Zenobia* (RSC, 1995); *In the Ruins* (Bristol Old Vic, 1990); *Food of Love* (Theatre de Complicité, 1988); *The Art of Success* (RSC, 1986); *Pure Science* (RSC, 1986); and *Temptation* (RSC, 1984). He also collaborated with Peter Brook on the development of *Qui est là?* (Bouffes du Nord, 1996). His adaptations include *The Promise* (after Arbuzov, Tricycle, 2002); *Summerfolk* (after Gorky, RNT, 1999); *Le Bourgeois Gentilhomme* (after Molière, RNT, 1992); *The Last Days of Don Juan* (after Tirso de Molina, RSC, 1990); and *A Family Affair* (after Ostrovsky, Cheek by Jowl, 1988). His screenplays include *Persuasion*, *The Turn of the Screw*, *Cinderella*, *The Gambler* and the forthcoming BBC mini-series *Byron*. He has written the libretti for three operas: *The Palace in the Sky* (ENO/Hackney Empire, 2001); and *Siren Song* (1994) and *A Family Affair* (1993), both premièred at the Almeida Opera Festival. He has also written extensively for radio, beginning with his very first play, *Matter Permitted* (1980).

NICK DEAR

Power

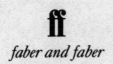

faber and faber

First published in 2003
by Faber and Faber Limited
3 Queen Square London WC1N 3AU
Published in the United States by Faber and Faber Inc.
an affiliate of Farrar, Straus and Giroux LLC, New York

Typeset by Country Setting, Kingsdown, Kent CT14 8ES
Printed in England by Mackays of Chatham plc, Chatham, Kent

A CIP record for this book
is available from the British Library

ISBN 0-571-22007-X

2 4 6 8 10 9 7 5 3 1

For Penny

Power was first presented at the Cottesloe Theatre on
3 July 2003 by the Royal National Theatre in association
with Vide Ulemek of Us Productions Ltd. The cast, in
order of speaking, was as follows:

Anne Barbara Jefford
Philippe Jonathan Slinger
Louis XIV Rupert Penry-Jones
Fouquet Robert Lindsay
Henriette Geraldine Somerville
Colbert Stephen Boxer
Louise Hattie Morahan

Director Lindsay Posner
Designer Chris Oram
Lighting Designer Wolfgang Goebbel
Music Michael Nyman
Sound Designer Neil Alexander
Director of Movement Peter Darling

Characters

Anne
Anne of Austria,
wife of the late Louis XIII, the Queen Mother.
Sixty

Louis
Louis XIV, King of France,
the 'Sun King'. Twenty-two

Philippe
Philippe, Duc d'Orléans,
brother of Louis, known at court as 'Monsieur'.
Twenty-one

Henriette
Henriette d'Angleterre,
daughter of the executed Charles I of England,
wife of Philippe, known at court as 'Madame'.
Twenty-five

Colbert
Jean-Baptiste Colbert, courtier. Forty-one

Fouquet
Nicolas Fouquet, courtier. Forty-five

Louise
Louise de La Vallière,
maid of honour to Madame. Sixteen

POWER

Act One

SCENE ONE

*March 1661. The Château de Vincennes, outside Paris.
Late night, a distant tolling bell. In an ante-room is Anne.*

Anne I learn my lessons from the lips of the dying: at
any moment they may come for us, knife scintillant in
the starlight, assassin sick with fear. So act first. Identify
the danger, disarm it, and destroy. (*She kisses a fabulous
ring on her finger. Very low and emotional.*) You have
taught me much.

Philippe enters.

Philippe Is he in there?

Anne Yes, but they won't let him stay. You know the
protocols. He may not look on the face of death. When
the Cardinal begins to fade, your brother will leave. They
will tell him.

Philippe But how will they know?

Anne They are physicians.

Philippe But what if, suddenly, the life deserts him?

Anne Your brother will look away.

Philippe In time, I hope.

Anne Of course in time. He is mindful of the protocols.

Philippe It would be awful if he made a mistake,
wouldn't it?

Anne He will make no mistakes. He will show due
respect. The Cardinal was our protector, and my dearest

friend. Through all the dark years, he did not desert us. I wear his gem. (*She fingers her ring.*) And now I shall pray for his soul. Come with me to the chapel.

Philippe I had hoped to view some fabrics that arrived very late. Some pretty brocatelle, I am assured.

Anne How can you think of your clothes at this time?

Philippe I'm about to be married, Mother. It's not exactly trivial.

Anne Well, I shall spend the night at prayer.

Philippe You think a vigil for his soul will be . . . productive?

Anne He perceives his insignificance in the eyes of God. He hopes for mercy. He has a fine sense of humility.

Philippe Yes, and a fantastic hoard of treasure.

Louis enters. He is pale.

Louis He's gone. Just minutes ago.

Anne (*breaking down*) Oh . . .!

Louis Be brave. (*He comforts Anne.*)

Philippe My condolence on the loss of your godfather.

Louis Thank you. I have given orders for the Devotions of the Forty Hours to be said in every church in Paris.

Philippe Only the sovereign should receive the Forty Hours!

Louis I've given my orders. And I've called my first Council.

Anne is curious.

Séguier, Fouquet, Lionne.

Anne The Cardinal's men. Good, I like continuity. Oh, my boys! (*She hugs them to her.*) The Cardinal is dead. Your father dead too. Now we are alone.

Louis I am scared.

Anne Go and see your brocades, Philippe. We excuse you.

Philippe (*kissing her hand*) Mother. (*to Louis*) I wish I could be of more use. But you know what I'm like.

Louis Philippe.

> *Louis hugs him close. Philippe bows, and exits. More bells have begun to toll. Anne sits.*

Anne You are not scared. I have bred courage into you. You are not scared. Now, are you settled on your First Minister?

Louis . . . The Cardinal spoke to me this morning.

Anne He was lucid?

Louis Yes. He's been living on partridge and opium pills, but he was lucid. He was led through the château, viewing for the final time his works of art. The Titian, the Correggios, the forty thousand volumes in the library, the twenty copies of the first printed Bible. 'I must leave all this!' he cried. 'I took such trouble to acquire it! Now I'll never see it again.' Oh, he was lucid. He said, 'The politicians are your servants, not your masters. Give place to no man. You alone are King.'

Anne What was he implying?

Louis It's quite clear. I must not be timid. I must establish my authority. I must judge my ministers solely on their merits.

Anne Did he say whom you can trust?

Louis He mentioned his secretary, Colbert.

Anne Colbert? The one who looks like a mole, burrowing through his ledgers? Who else?

Louis is silent.

What is on your mind, Louis?

Louis I am thinking I shall rule personally.

Anne Kings do not do that. We have help.

Louis But kings can be led by their creatures. I will not be controlled by a favourite. Instinct tells me I should rule France on my own.

Anne Instinct? Pah! How is instinct going to help you run a country? You are not conversant with the economics!

Louis And why not? Because the state accounts are kept secret! How can I govern if I don't know my own financial position?

Anne My darling boy. It will be hard.

Louis Will you give me your blessing, Mother?

Anne Gladly.

Louis kneels to kiss her hand.

Louis (*softly*) My heart pounds in my chest. If I get it wrong . . .

Anne If you get it wrong there are plenty of men with ancient scores to settle. Oh, they kneel and beg, but their entreaties veil their true agenda: royal blood. Our blood. Crowned heads on poles, and ploughboys at play with our entrails. Stand up, Louis; be firm.

Louis You have always told me how to act. You and Mazarin. But now I must make my own law. I don't know if I . . . know enough!

Anne You were born to be King. No further qualifications are required.

Louis And yet –

Anne Look, what precisely concerns you?

Louis We have no money!

Anne Pah. We have never had money.

Louis It's embarrassing!

Anne No. One will not be embarrassed.

Louis But my brother is to marry the poor English princess without a father, and I have to provide her dowry, and how am I supposed to do that?

Anne Borrow.

Louis Go crawling to financiers?

Anne They must help us. God made us greater than them. Monsieur Fouquet has obliged in the past. Apply to him.

Louis Fouquet – that's a good idea.

Anne Monsieur Fouquet is a very gifted fellow. He throws the most wonderful parties. He surrounds himself with poets, playwrights, painters, men of science. His table's the most sumptuous in France, his politics the most urbane. And now that Mazarin is gone – may heaven safeguard him – he is the wealthiest man in the kingdom. Should he not be First Minister?

Louis Why must I do it the old way?

Anne Because that's the way that it's done!

Louis Fouquet's candidacy isn't in question. But must I really follow antiquated systems?

Anne What is this, progress? You know my views on progress.

Louis I am no radical, Mother. But I want improvements. I seek a perfection of government. I want my subjects to applaud.

Anne . . . For years they tried to kill us. The subjects. Remember? Now power is regained. Do let's not throw it away.

Louis We will see.

They exit. The bells toll all across Paris.

SCENE TWO

Water meadows. Fouquet enters, equipped for hawking, wearing a buckskin gauntlet and high leather boots: the height of fashion. He is at a run, his eyes on the sky. Dogs are yapping.

Fouquet There he goes! He is rising!

Louis (*off*) Are the hawks on?

Fouquet They close! He has seen them!

Louis enters running. He too is dressed for the hunt.

Louis Where?

Fouquet There!

Louis They seem to fly in different directions!

Fouquet They're spiralling, to try to get above him! Remember, never pitch a hawk too low!

Louis I'll remember.

Fouquet The heron mounts higher and higher!

Louis Will we bring him down?

Fouquet (*laughs*) A heron's no match for my longwings, Majesty.

Louis What a cast of birds!

Fouquet I trained them myself. Would you like them? They're yours! – Look, the first makes her stoop!

Louis The heron shifts –

Fouquet He's disgorged his food – the second dives –

Louis The heron shakes her off! Have we lost him?

Fouquet No, it's a good flight, they'll rise and stoop again!

Louis What a height they climb to!

  They shade their eyes to watch the soaring birds.

Fouquet Of course, those I have reared myself are rather dearer than the ones trained by my falconer. I doubt I could let one of them go for – what? – much less than fifty.

Louis (*crestfallen*) Fifty thousand livres? For a falcon?

Fouquet Plus the gauntlets, the hoods, the jesses and the lures . . .

Louis I think I'll stick to billiards.

Fouquet I joke, Majesty, I jest, I jape. They are my gift to you.

Louis Oh. Well, thank you very much, Fouquet.

Fouquet Don't mention it.

Louis For a moment I thought you were serious.

Fouquet Me? Serious?

  Louis laughs. He likes Fouquet.

Louis You are not like the others.

Fouquet The other what? Bird-fanciers?

Louis No, the other men of money. You've a free and easy way of doing business. To be honest, you are almost rude. Were I to come to you with a small request, I feel sure we would still go along in friendship, wouldn't we?

Fouquet (*smiles*) How may I assist you, Majesty?

Louis I believe you've on occasion helped my mother with a loan.

Fouquet Ah, she's told you of the Siege of Valenciennes, in the dreadful days of the Fronde? How much do you recall of the rebellion? Your troops were on the point of mutiny. 'The Queen must have money,' said Mazarin to me, 'ready money!' So I went, cap in hand, to my family and friends, and found nearly a million livres, in four days flat! I shipped it to your army in handcarts. I bent my shoulder to the yoke on rutted roads. How much do you want?

Louis My brother's marrying next month . . . I have to provide the girl's dowry . . . if we *can* agree terms . . .

Fouquet Terms? For Nicolas Fouquet there are no terms, no nasty, smudgy little papers. A handshake is sufficient.

Louis smiles with relief and they clasp hands.

Eighteen per cent all right?

Louis I thought you said –

Fouquet (*triumphantly*) Got him again!

Louis (*grins*) Eighteen per cent's not legal, is it?

Fouquet I tell you what, *I'm* the Superintendent of Finance, you let me worry about that. (*He scans the sky.*) They're harrying him, look! That old heron's tired . . .

Louis I could always cancel the wedding. The expense makes me wonder if it's worth it.

Fouquet No, that would be unwise. Forging ties with England is expedient, now the Stuarts are back. The rabble have been vanquished, although pathetically hard work was made of it, one fails to see why it took eighteen years, and the bride-to-be's brother has at last reclaimed his throne. What is he, your cousin?

Louis nods.

Pay for the wedding, and he becomes your friend.

Louis Good point. King Charles will be a useful ally.

Fouquet Who knows, he may last longer than his father.

Louis (*looking up*) They're on to him! They've got him!

Fouquet The second hawk binds to the first!

Louis They fall so slowly! Their frenzied wings!

They watch as the birds clatter to the ground. The dogs start up a commotion. Fouquet calls to their handlers.

Fouquet Slip the dogs!

Louis It's thrilling!

Fouquet (*grins*) You just have to climb higher than your prey. – He's downed! – Now for the hard part, Majesty. Now to get the hunters home. You have your hood?

Fouquet takes his falcon's hood from his bag, and some raw meat.

Like this. We entice them to us, then hood them.

Louis Why?

Fouquet The bird experiences the world through her eyes. If she can't see it, it doesn't exist. Once in the hood, she's safe, and compliant. (*Sighs.*) If only catching women was that simple . . .

Louis (*grins*) I'm a married man, Fouquet.

Fouquet Fundamentally no obstacle. The purpose of a wife is to remind us what we're missing.

Louis And what has yours reminded you of, lately?

Fouquet (*conspiratorially*) I have my eye on a little one, recently come to court – delicious. She resists. But I will enchant her. – Come, let's catch these beauties, then I'll give you a game of billiards.

Louis (*leaving*) I'll beat you, Monsieur!

Fouquet Yes, you may do.

Louis exits towards the birds holding out a handful of raw meat. Fouquet smiles indulgently, and follows.

SCENE THREE

Some weeks later. The gardens at Fontainebleau. A lovely day. Distant music. Henriette strolls with Philippe. He wears extravagant clothes and lots of make-up. He waves to his friends.

Henriette My, my – you are very much the centre of attention.

Philippe I should certainly hope so. Otherwise all those hours in the boudoir must be counted a mistake.

Henriette I know I am new to the court, and perhaps have yet to learn its ways. But is it considered normal for a gentleman to sit with his wife's maids, in his under-things, posing and pouting and caking pigments and powders on his cheeks?

Philippe Depends who you ask, really.

Henriette But you chatter with these girls as an intimate! You, a prince of the blood! – But as I say, I am new.

Philippe In matters of complexion, no one knows more than a fifteen-year-old virgin. I am ever eager for advice.

Henriette And the ribbons? And the stockings?

Philippe Henriette, you know why this match was arranged: no one else would have me, and no one else would have you, dear heart.

Henriette But some of your practices will have to be curtailed, if we are to spend the rest of our lives together.

Philippe The rest of our lives? I'm done in after barely a fortnight.

Henriette How very gallant of you.

Philippe Oh, you know what I mean. We gave the world a wedding. The spectacle was lush. But I confess the novelty of being a husband has rather worn off. I belong with my own sort, really.

Henriette With the Chevalier de Lorraine? The Comte de Guiche? They are pretty but their lips are cruel.

Philippe I think they are utterly angelic. (*He waves to more friends.*) Before you appeared I was the sole object of their adulation. I was fêted and adored, as is fit and proper. But recently I have had cause to remark that your ankles receive more attention than my own.

Henriette (*laughs*) The Comte de Guiche has a gift for flattery. Which is lucky, as I can't see what else he's good for.

Philippe This is not to be borne! I cannot tolerate it! I did not marry to acquire a rival!

Henriette What did you marry for, then?

Philippe It is my duty, obviously!

Henriette What do you want me to do? Sit in the Tuileries, listening to the mice? I am young!

Philippe The Queen is young. *She* sets a first-class example.

Henriette She is big with child.

Philippe At least she has the manners not to show herself about.

Henriette Spanish manners. She retires at eight o'clock after an exciting game of spillikins, and gets up at daybreak for Mass. She is never seen in public and His Majesty, I fancy, dines out more often than at home. He might like something lighter than that meaty garlic stew.

Philippe Madame, your tongue runs ahead of you.

Henriette I can only wish yours did, Monsieur.

Philippe I see the maids of honour by the pavilion. They will not insult me. I shall laugh and talk and be happy. Please do not follow and spoil it.

Philippe bows cordially and exits. After a moment Henriette flops to the ground, not very decorously.

Henriette Oh, piss.

She lies back, fed up. Louis enters. He stands aside, listening.

Henriette Where on earth have I ended up? Nobody's very diverting, at all. They just strut about like chessmen that have fallen from the board. And the place is an absolute wilderness!

Louis I am sorry, Madame, you have contrived such a low opinion of the gardens of Fontainebleau. Customarily it is where we come to hunt.

Henriette jumps up in embarrassment, and curtsies low.

Henriette My tongue runs ahead of me, Majesty.

Louis (*indicating the garden*) How would you improve it?

Henriette It is hardly for me to speculate that your Majesty's holdings might be improved.

Louis But fiddling with the landscape is so very much in fashion. I should quite like to hear your views.

Henriette . . . It might be nice if things were a little more ornamental. Some parterres, a water-feature or two. A little more feminine, shall we say?

Louis Is that how they do it in England?

Henriette I haven't lived in England since I was young.

Louis Ah, no. A bad business, your father. Sends a chill down every Frenchman's spine.

Louis sits on the grass. Henriette remains standing.

So. You don't find my brother diverting? We all love him, you know.

Henriette Monsieur is at all times charming and agreeable, Majesty.

Louis But not diverting.

Henriette Not . . . perhaps . . . in all the ways a lady might wish to be diverted.

Louis You have wit, Madame. We are honoured to have you among us.

Henriette I am grateful for your hospitality, Majesty, as I have nowhere else to go.

Louis Well, as your host, how may I make your residence here more amenable? What do you like to do?

Henriette I like to play the spinet, I like to dance . . .

Louis I like to dance.

Henriette I like the theatre very much.

Louis Do you? I like it too.

Henriette Corneille is awfully fine.

Louis Molière also.

Henriette Molière? Is that Monsieur Fouquet's man?

Louis Yes, Fouquet's man. Makes me laugh, though some people think him facetious. Will you sit with me?

Henriette That is too great an honour.

Louis But I wish it.

Henriette They are watching us.

Louis Sit.

Henriette sits next to him.

I often feel I am an actor in a play. The play is called *The Reign of Louis the Fourteenth*. (*Smiles.*) I am the hero, of course.

Henriette You play it expertly.

Louis I am still learning my lines.

Henriette Does Her Majesty the Queen take a part?

Louis A significant part, but offstage much of the time.

Henriette Then who is your leading lady?

Louis Yet to be cast. I am thinking of holding auditions.

Henriette (*laughs*) You are having fun with me.

Louis Yes, I am. (*He looks into her eyes.*) I watch you. You have spirit. Your teeth are good, your eyes bright.

Henriette You make me sound like a thoroughbred.

Louis (*smiles*) Few would have the nerve to say that.

Henriette I am not like other women.

Louis No, you stand several hands taller.

Henriette (*laughs*) I don't take a bridle very well.

Louis I'm sure you are the perfect mount. (*Pause.*) Madame. (*Pause.*) Are you angry?

Henriette No, I'm trying not to break out in a sweat.

Louis You have yet to be ridden. How could you sweat?

Henriette . . . Perhaps your Majesty would care to come for a canter tomorrow?

> *Colbert enters, keeping to the side. He has spectacles, and always wears black. He carries a ledger.*

Louis Monsieur Colbert.

> *Colbert bows to Louis and Henriette. They stand.*

Colbert May I address your Majesty on an urgent matter?

> *Louis indicates that he may. They move aside. Henriette is completely ignored.*

Concerning the estate of Cardinal Mazarin: I have located certain sums of money, hidden –

Louis Where?

Colbert At Vincennes, at Brissac, La Fère, Sedan –

Louis How much?

Colbert A total . . . (*Consults his ledger.*) in the order of nineteen million livres.

Louis Good God.

Colbert No mention is made of these concealed funds in his will. His heirs are provided for. It appears, on scrutinising the documents, that, er, his Eminence's purpose was that these monies should accrue to the Crown. For your personal use.

Louis Who else knows of this?

Colbert Myself alone.

Louis Superintendent Fouquet?

Colbert No.

Louis Why not?

Colbert I thought you should hear it first.

Louis . . . This will grant me a degree of independence.

Colbert Yes. And there is much to be done. The treasury is in considerable disarray.

Louis Is it? Who's responsible?

Colbert I won't make malicious accusations. But you will not be unacquainted with the luxurious style of life of your ministers – whilst the Royal Works founder for want of money, buildings are left incomplete, the Louvre barely furnished . . . why, at times we have been in want of a pair of silver candlesticks for your Majesty's bedroom!

Louis I had noticed.

Colbert If I may make bold, our, er, the project is to dazzle the world with the effortless superiority of our culture. France has the best of everything. But we are tied in knots by financiers, and usury at four hundred per cent, and tax-farmers who skim off not just the cream but half the milk as well. The gross tax revenue for this year is eighty-six million livres; that is what the treasury ought to expect. How much does it receive? About fifty million.

Louis As little as that? Why?

Colbert Without sight of the accounts, it's, er, it's rather hard to say.

Louis I have confidence in Monsieur Fouquet.

Colbert Oh, so do I. He is rightly lauded for his fiscal abilities. But surely, blessed with people of such talent, the country should be turning a profit? We have the scientists, the artists, the diplomats, the builders. Conditions for trade are ideal. After years of war, we are at peace. There is no dissent in the land.

Louis There is famine.

Colbert Famine, yes, but no dissent – it is a real opportunity! A new age is waiting to dawn, a tremendous aurora, rising up! We lack but one thing: capital.

Louis I am glad you've come to me, Colbert. But what should I do?

Colbert We must lay hold of the accounts, Majesty. The profit and loss of the nation cannot be sealed and secreted. Information is power.

Louis Agreed.

Colbert When you have concise information, the path ahead will be clear.

Louis I am thinking I should like you to go and work with Superintendent Fouquet. Assist him in his labours. See what you can learn.

Colbert Thank you, Majesty.

Louis Thank you, Monsieur.

Colbert bows and leaves. Henriette is waiting patiently. Louis smiles at her.

Henriette Who is that man?

Louis A merchant, from a long line of merchants.

Henriette I don't like him much.

Louis It is not necessary to like him.

Louis exits, his mind on business. Henriette curtsies.

Henriette . . . Is it necessary to like me, I wonder?

SCENE FOUR

Fouquet's house at Saint-Mandé. Colbert works at a desk piled high with ledgers and papers. Candles are guttering. Fouquet enters in his nightshirt, with a bottle of champagne.

Fouquet Jean-Baptiste, you have been here fourteen hours.

Colbert Yes, I shall leave soon.

Fouquet It is the dead of night. Do you never stop?

Colbert Cross-checking two more entries, then I'll be off home. We must be in good order for the coming round of talks with the taxmen.

Fouquet (*aside*) What a thoughtful fellow the King turns out to be. He knows I am busy with plans and programmes, schemes and salons, so he kindly provides a comrade for the dull diurnal round. – I do have clerks, you know.

Colbert I believe if you want a thing done properly, you have to do it yourself.

Fouquet Take a glass of champagne with me.

Colbert I prefer water to wine, thank you, Superintendent.

Fouquet Everybody I know likes a drink. Your sobriety makes you look suspicious.

Colbert Well, that's unfortunate. I am what I am.

Fouquet What are you hoping to find? Evidence of illegality?

Colbert No, I am just here to assist, I'm sure nothing like that will turn up.

Fouquet Everything I do is illegal.

Colbert (*shocked*) Is it?

Fouquet Oh, technically, technically. Little crimes in the service of the King.

Colbert I find that hard to believe.

Fouquet Don't play the innocent, Jean-Baptiste. We both learnt the trade under the late Cardinal. You know as well as I do that if we can't milk the system we deserve to be tilling the fields.

Colbert Well, your star is in the ascendant.

Fouquet Because I can do magic. The magic of money. I am a wizard with money, a warlock of finance, a necromancer of the numismatic arts!

Colbert They are calling you the power behind the throne.

Fouquet (*delighted*) Are they?

Colbert Yes. I often wonder how you, er, how you have gained such influence . . . ?

Fouquet slurps his champagne.

Fouquet Well, the King is not rich, is he? His estates yield – what? – eighty thousand a year? Birdseed. And because the treasury collapsed when he was a boy, it's not easy for him to raise funds – banks won't lend to a head of state with no collateral, and on the verge of bankruptcy. So he has to turn to his friends, good friends like myself.

Colbert That doesn't sound illegal to me.

Fouquet No, it isn't, it isn't, only in the detail.

Colbert So your gift is in raising ready money?

Fouquet My gift is in raising ready money, on my personal debentures, and with this I fill the King's coffers. Naturally it is understood that a financier must be reimbursed for these advances, even possibly with a thimbleful of interest. And thus the system survives, the mechanics of government grind and hiss from reign to reign to reign . . . It is the ancient way, and the ancient ways are best, don't you agree? I am the loyalest of subjects. I would protect my sovereign with my dying breath. I'd be an arse not to. The only thing that surpasses my joy in making money is the delight I take in spending it.

Colbert (*gazing round*) Yes.

Fouquet I love luxury and refinement. I live for beauty and pleasure, I live among dew-speckled flowers, Gobelin tapestries, a consort of viols. I collect rare manuscripts, statues, porcelains, coins. I've just bought half-a-dozen warships from the Dutch. I have a laboratory where a philosopher called Pecquet tracks the circulation of the blood. I have my artists and my writers and my friends are numbered among the great and the good. I am building a palace at Vaux-le-Vicomte! But I don't want to talk about that. It's a surprise, for my good friend the King. He likes surprises, doesn't he?

Colbert I do not share with His Majesty the degree of intimacy that you do.

Fouquet Sometimes I worry that I'm being overlooked. Why aren't I already First Minister? Sometimes I get terribly troubled. (*He seems suddenly dejected.*)

Colbert There, I am finished. (*Colbert packs away his quills and ledgers.*) Why do you so want to be First Minister? Haven't you, er, haven't you got enough?

Fouquet Why do I want to be First Minister? (*He ponders.*) Why does a God who has made a man still want to create a woman? – sorry, is that blasphemous? Sorry. Why does a man who's drunk two bottles of champagne still want to uncork a third? Why does a buck rabbit, having fathered a thousand bunnies, still want to fuck anything with floppy ears? Who is better equipped to be First Minister than me?

Colbert That's a very good question, and though I shall ponder it all the way home, I doubt I shall formulate an answer.

Fouquet Look, why exactly are you here?

Colbert I told you. I was sent to assist.

Fouquet But I didn't need assisting.

Colbert (*laughs*) Oh, I think, er, having seen your books – well, let's agree to differ on that one, shall we?

Fouquet You are not spying on me, Jean-Baptiste?

Colbert If I was, I should be nervous. But I'm not.

Fouquet So your interest is solely in the accounts?

Colbert I don't find much else in life meaningful, Superintendent.

Fouquet relaxes. He pours himself more champagne.
He cheers up.

Fouquet Can you make them look credible?

Colbert Oh, yes. People will believe anything if the handwriting's neat enough.

Fouquet Then we'll see you again tomorrow, shall we?

Colbert You shall. Goodnight.

Colbert bows and leaves. Fouquet drinks. He is thoughtful.

SCENE FIVE

The Château of Fontainebleau. Louis, Anne, Philippe. Philippe is wearing a dress. They are all angry.

Louis I am mindful of the proprieties.

Anne But are you mindful of your salvation? Are you mindful of the peril in which you walk?

Louis Yes I am!

Anne I think you are intoxicated by your own glory. I think, being as you believe all-powerful, entrusted with this monarchy by God, you recognise no limits to your base desires!

Louis I fulfil my obligations, all of them!

Anne We know that.

Louis So what exactly is the problem?

Philippe (*stamping his foot*) She's my wife, damn it!

They both turn and look at him. He's flustered.

Oh, you know what I mean. It makes a fellow feel dreadfully small, when his brother goes on picnics with his wife.

Louis Picnics! They are picnics!

Anne You go bathing together!

Louis It's been hot!

Anne Oh, I despair of you, Louis! This must cease. The Queen is in tears. The court is reverberant with rumour. You cannot conduct an *affaire* with Madame!

Louis We discuss poetry and music. She is a rare thing at court: she has a mind of her own. We dance; we drive in the forest. It is hardly an *affaire*!

Anne The Queen regards it as infidelity. To her – in her confinement – it is one more example of the very lax morals of the French. I am inclined to say I agree with her.

Louis You're her aunt! Naturally you agree with her!

Anne And look at poor Philippe. He is jealous, poor lamb. He won't even dance any more.

Louis Only because I get more applause than he does.

Anne Why must you be so competitive? Haven't I done everything possible to ensure he is no threat? Haven't I dressed him in frocks and bonnets from the age of three, and left him to play with the ladies, so you will never be tempted to garrotte him in his sleep? Why do you think he is like this? Because I will it. And my will is stronger than yours. Come to your senses!

Louis . . . I apologise, Mother. I try to avoid surrendering to my passions, but sometimes they overcome my reason.

Anne I see. Well, you must at least disguise it. It cannot go on in the open.

Philippe Mother . . .

Anne Be quiet. I will speak to Henriette. You will be apprised of the arrangements. Come, Philippe.

Anne and Philippe exit. Louis kicks at the furniture in youthful frustration.

Louis Well, this is hardly the absolute power of which I do confess I dream!

Colbert enters and bows.

What do you want?

Colbert Majesty, with the greatest respect, I want the royal line to prosper, I want never to return to the anarchy of the Fronde.

Louis I'm not in the mood. Be brief.

Colbert My research indicates that all departments of state should be brought under centralised control.

Louis Agreed.

Colbert In the first instance I would recommend a reform of the Exchequer.

Louis Why? Monsieur Fouquet is an effective Superintendent.

Colbert He is also an effective Vicomte de Melun, Marquis de Belle-Isle, and Attorney General to the Parliament of Paris. He has something too much power.

Louis He helps me! He teaches me! And you say he is a threat?

Colbert I don't think, Majesty, I said anything of the kind. I am simply suggesting a fresh look at policy at ministerial level.

Louis Do you bear some grudge against Fouquet?

Colbert I bear no grudge against anybody. But he has made himself a fortune in ten years.

Louis But he's gifted, he's clever. He deserves it! Are we forbidden to enrich ourselves now?

Colbert No, Majesty, but I am veering to the hypothesis that he has enriched himself to the detriment of, and at the, er, expense of the state.

Louis Just a minute, he's my friend! Your evidence?

Colbert I have none.

Louis On thin ice, then, aren't you, Colbert?

Colbert I am well aware that your Majesty could find these conjectures unpalatable, and terminate our intimacy, on which I dare to presume only from some precepts of loyalty and service. I serve France. You are France.

Pause. Louis looks French. Colbert steels himself to continue.

Colbert And in France it is illegal to borrow at interest of more than five and five-ninths per cent, I expect you know this? But to raise ready money, for the state's usage, the Superindent might have to offer twelve, or fifteen, or twenty per cent! So – if he writes down anything at all – he writes down the capital sum as far greater than it is, and then invents expenses to balance the books. Whose expenses? Why, his!

Louis But this kind of thing goes on all the time, doesn't it? Fouquet isn't a *criminal*! What has made you so suspicious of the man?

Colbert Majesty, the world is built on numbers. I collate and analyze them. That's all. I look at the figures and draw my conclusions. In the Department of Justice, for example, there are forty-six thousand offices. Of these, forty thousand were created simply to be sold! And those people don't pay tax! Now, expressed as a percentage of the adult population, that's –

Louis I've heard enough!

Louis storms out.

SCENE SIX

Fouquet walks with Anne through the gardens of the Tuileries.

Fouquet He absorbs information like a sponge. We have several times discussed foreign policy, and I must say he seems perfectly at ease among the tangled matrices of international relations. Economic policy he needn't worry himself with overmuch.

Anne Why not?

Fouquet Because I was placed on earth by God to panic for him.

Anne (*laughs*) Well, we are lucky to have you, Monsieur.

Fouquet Your Majesty's praise is a shaft of sunlight shot through a sleet-grey sky; it illumines our lives with its lustre. – Majesty, good morning!

Louis passes through. Fouquet bows.

Louis Mother. (*He bows to her.*)

Anne I am told you are learning fast.

Louis That's because I've an excellent tutor. A man with a great lust for life.

Fouquet Thank you, Majesty. But I do sometimes grow melancholic – not unlike, as I believe, many great men, out of office . . .

Louis Well, I've never seen it. (*Turns to leave, then turns back*.) Oh, there is something I'd like you to do.

Fouquet Anything, Majesty.

Louis I've decided I want a complete inventory of the Treasury.

Fouquet With the greatest pleasure, Majesty, but Majesty, that hasn't – to be blunt – that hasn't been required for many years.

Louis Exactly why I'd like you to compile it.

Fouquet I do not comprehensively understand . . .

Louis There is criticism, Monsieur, you have critics in the world. I could dispel their innuendoes more severely were I armed with a set of accounts.

Fouquet Criticism?

Louis It surprised me, too. But do the audit, there's a good fellow. Then, when the air is clear, you may take up your rightful position.

Louis smiles warmly at Fouquet, bows to Anne and leaves.

Fouquet Is it Colbert, do you think? This *critic*?

Anne I hardly know him. Do you?

Fouquet Oh, I know him. Our differences are summed up by the symbols on our shields. Mine is a charming little squirrel, my motto '*Quo non ascendam*,' 'How high might I not climb?' – 'Fouquet' meaning 'squirrel' in the old Breton tongue. Colbert's arms sport a rather slimy grass-snake, *coluberta* in Latin. He says it stands for prudence. God knows what his motto is. I can barely believe the King trusts him!

Anne Sometimes you have to work with people you don't trust.

Fouquet Am I to be First Minister?

Anne He says your candidacy is not in question.

Fouquet And my 'rightful position'? What's that?

Anne Have faith, Monsieur. We like you.

*Anne turns briskly from him and goes on her way.
Fouquet bows.*

Fouquet They like me. Thank God. I am liked. (*He exits.*)

SCENE SEVEN

*Henriette's apartment at the Tuileries. She sits, waiting.
Louis enters, making sure he is unobserved. She runs to
him and they embrace.*

Louis (*apologetically*) Matters of state.

Henriette (*kissing him*) I am used to waiting. I have
waited and waited. And now my life is, I have to say
it is idyllic! It was so hard before!

They sit, holding hands.

Louis Was it?

Henriette We went from château to château, on the coat-
tails of the court. To be the daughter of an executed king
is not a great introduction to society.

Louis How did you survive?

Henriette My mother begged and borrowed. I darned my
own stockings! Can you imagine that?

Louis I don't expect you darn them now.

Henriette I wear them once – and then when they are
off – they are off!

Louis What – completely off?

Henriette My legs are bare.

Louis I think you'll have to demonstrate. I don't quite understand.

Henriette Not now, I can't do it now.

Louis Yes you can.

Henriette I can't!

Louis It's only a scene in a play.

Henriette No it isn't!

Louis Can't we discuss your legs?

Henriette No!

Louis Discourse on your long, hot thighs? Explore your equatorial regions?

Henriette Not this morning, no.

Louis (*hand up her skirts*) What do my cartographers call this new terrain?

Henriette Disputed territory.

Louis You fear the breaching of its borders by the mighty sword of France?

Henriette No, but I was granted – no, no, no, no!

She fends him off. He sulks.

I was granted an audience with the Queen Mother.

Louis (*sighs*) Oh, I see.

Henriette Her Majesty was quite forceful. She says I can't continue making open liaisons with you. She proposed a variety of forfeits . . . a goose-farm in Gascony was mentioned . . .

Louis Yes, it often is.

Henriette I like her. A redoubtable woman –

Louis Yes, yes.

Henriette – who threatened me terribly. So what we have devised is this: when you come to see me you will not be coming to see me, you will be coming to see one of my maids of honour, with whom you have fallen inexplicably in love. Your mother lined them all up and chose her. Her name is Louise Le Blanc La Baume, Demoiselle de La Vallière, and she comes from the country. Which bit precisely escapes me, father a cavalryman or something. Not exactly of the stock of kings, our Louise. Still, she will do what she's told, and give it out to the court that your Majesty and she are in love.

Louis This really is excrutiatingly tedious. I was hoping to –

Henriette Please, oh, please, it's only so that you and I can meet! I long to swim with you again, to wrap myself around you in the water . . . Come to my apartments, ask for Louise de La Vallière, she receives you, she promptly fades like the morning mist, and in her place you find . . . your Henriette.

Louis But what is she like, this girl? Pretty?

Henriette Pretty, but no personality at all. Entirely credible as a royal mistress. See for yourself! (*Rings a bell.*) Your mother has contrived it splendidly!

Louise enters. She has lovely platinum hair, a good figure, and a limp. Beautiful but very shy.

His Majesty King Louis.

Henriette exits. Louis motions for Louise to sit. She does so, staring at the floor, terrified. He circles her.

Louis A virgin?

She nods.

Been holding on, have we? Despite the depredations of
the chevaliers?

She nods.

So, never had a cock between your thighs . . .

Louise I'm not sure it is polite to speak like that.

Louis No, it isn't. I'm sorry.

Louise I don't mind. You are angry.

Louis . . . I don't suppose I should be angry with you.

Louise Thank you, Majesty. You do me too much
honour.

Louis Oh, God, honour – this is all about honour.
I cannot be seen to be sleeping with my brother's wife.
But I can be seen to be sleeping with you.

Louise Thank you very much, Majesty.

Louis Don't mention it. (*Pause.*) You are nervous?

Louise I don't want to do anything you might disapprove
of.

Louis I admire your attitude, Mademoiselle, but in the
present context I suggest you revise it.

Louise . . . I should do something improper?

Louis I think it's expected of you.

Louise Why, Majesty?

Louis Weren't you told? What did they say?

Louise They said I'd a special appointment. They said to
brush my hair.

Louis Your hair is lovely.

Louise Thank you, Majesty.

Louis If I tell you to stop thanking me will you do so?

Louise Yes, Majesty, thank you.

Louis And you'll carry out my orders without question?

Louise To the letter. What should I do?

Louis (*smiles*) We will see.

Louise I can *try* to be improper, but I may need some instruction.

Louis Your age?

Louise Sixteen.

Louis Let me look. (*He puts his fingertips under her chin, and tilts her head back. His fingers linger on her neck.*) Where are you from, Louise?

Louise From the Touraine, Majesty.

Louis You have not been long at court?

Louise A few weeks only.

Louis Fattened up and sent to market, eh?

Louise Not *too* fat, I hope.

Louis Oh goodness me no. Not too fat at all.

SCENE EIGHT

Moments later. Henriette is pacing outside her own apartment.

Henriette Why is it taking so long? What are they whispering about?

Fouquet passes nearby, dressed exquisitely, and carrying a small ornamented case.

Monsieur Fouquet?

Fouquet (*bowing*) Madame, your beauty is unsurpassed in France, your charms acclaimed from your Brest to your Pyrenees.

Henriette Where did you learn to flatter like that? Do they run courses in it?

Fouquet I am insensible of any flattery, Madame. I speak as I find.

Henriette How do you come to be in my private apartments, Monsieur?

He is silent.

The look in your eye, the gift in your grasp, suggest a man bent on seduction.

Fouquet Were I a brave man, a bold man, a knight sure in the saddle, I would pursue you through the deepest penumbra of the palace of the Louvre, until you yielded to my vehement advance – which is a train of thought so abject, not to say treasonable, that I think it only once or twice *per diem*.

She smiles.

But, alas, I am old. Look at me. This is my own hair. Oh, you will express surprise, but I assure you it is bracken now, where once it was a forest! Oh, the timber that the years have cut from me! The wretched logging-camp that is my life!

She laughs.

But, silviculture aside, let us just say I have not the humour for a mighty assignation, being no more the sturdy swain of yesteryear, but a worn-out servant of the

35

state and its Exchequer. I seek a light confection of the passions on a heady summer's eve, a timbale of sensation, not – God I feel decrepit saying this – not the full meal of lust, the nine-course banquet of desire, desserts of venery drenched in cream, the death by a thousand little deaths that is a satyr's dinner, no! – my heart couldn't stand it, and anyway I doubt you are free.

She shakes her head.

Word has it you are not. So I've my bloodshot eye on a surrogate.

Henriette What's in the box?

Fouquet Oh, this? (*He opens it.*) An apricot.

Henriette (*amazed*) An apricot?

Fouquet From my hothouse at Vaux-le-Vicomte. Propagated the thing myself, mingled its seed with my own two hands, teased it into moist and juicy being. It is for her. For Louise.

Henriette Louise?

Fouquet La Vallière. The object of my ardour.

Henriette I count the Demoiselle de La Vallière among my household –

Fouquet – where the erotic education she receives is unparalleled in Paris, yes, that is why I would give her my gift.

Henriette Her affections lie elsewhere.

Fouquet Of course, only natural, but –

Henriette She is in love.

Fouquet – fundamentally no obstacle. I should still be pleased to offer up my fruit.

Henriette (*barring his way*) I cannot allow you to enter, Superintendent. (*Beat.*) She is with her lover.

Fouquet A rival? – If he's over thirty I'll challenge him.

Henriette There will be no duels under my roof. And he's not over thirty.

Fouquet A young man . . . ! Young men are heedless of the riches they hold in their hands, the true value of ripening flesh, the succulence of innocence . . .

Henriette Are they really.

Fouquet They are, they are! It is only with the burden of years, with the getting of wisdom both fiscal and carnal – do you mind me talking like this? – that we begin to envision the perfection we have lost, to appreciate the audacious loveliness of our first fucks. – You don't mind, do you? – I'm a rich man, but let us just say that nothing can recover me the thrill of those first fumblings, those offerings up in kitchens of little furtive kisses, those edgings apart, on steamy nights, of wilful wayward knees . . . Only a man with thinning hair can know the truth of this. Indeed only a man with an apricot.

Henriette I don't care how fruity you are. You're not going in.

Fouquet Who is it?

Henriette I can't say.

Fouquet Yes you can. Come on.

Henriette No, I can't!

Fouquet Some consider me powerful, you know.

Henriette Some consider him powerful, too.

37

Fouquet My brain riffles through the index but it can't locate a match. Who is this lofty paramour of she whom I adore?

Henriette I am not at liberty to say! Please leave.

Fouquet (*turning to go*) . . . My intelligence has it you are close with the King.

Henriette We speak.

Fouquet Speak to him of me. I await an appointment which he has – curiously – yet to confirm. Plus there is this bizarre request for an inventory . . . and the subtle infiltrations of my old friend Jean-Baptiste, the snake in the grass, the collater of data . . . What, I wonder, does go on?

She remains non-committal. He retreats.

At least say I am witty; where's the compromise in that?

Henriette (*smiles*) There is none.

Fouquet (*bowing*) Madame. – Oh, would you present the lascivious Louise with the spawn of my sweat-soaked garden? (*He gives her the box.*)

Exit Fouquet. Henriette paces, eyeing the apricot. At length she picks it up and takes a bite out of it. Louis enters from within, smiling to himself.

Louis What have you there?

Henriette An apricot.

Louis (*taking it*) How rare and unusual.

Henriette Like me.

Louis Do you know I have never eaten one?

Henriette Did you finalise the details?

Louis Absolutely, yes. I'm sure it will all go according to plan.

He turns to leave. Henriette catches his arm.

Henriette Won't you kiss me?

Louis Why, with pleasure.

They kiss.

You taste strange.

Henriette I taste of apricot.

Louis (*laughing*) Oh, I see.

He exits, taking a bite from the apricot. Henriette heads inside, angrily.

SCENE NINE

The Louvre. Shadows and torches. Anne passes through with Colbert.

Colbert Every day his dossiers are handed to the King. Every evening in my sanctum I devour them. We wind but trudgingly uphill. We are still at the foot of the mountain. When we stand on the summit, and view the full range of his rapacity –

Anne Come to the point. Please.

Colbert The Cardinal was on the verge of arresting Fouquet shortly before he died.

Anne No he wasn't. For what?

Colbert Treason.

Anne I don't believe it. Monsieur Fouquet has always been loyal.

Colbert Majesty, the Cardinal discovered a paper, wherein is detailed the Superintendent's plans to retreat, should he be disgraced, to Brittany – from there to launch attacks upon the offices of France.

Anne Rot! Continue.

Colbert The island of Belle-Isle, at the mouth of Quiberon Bay, was purchased from the Duc de Retz by the Superintendent.

Anne (*wearily*) We know that. Cardinal Mazarin sanctioned it, as a token of our gratitude.

Colbert You know Fouquet's fortified it? You know he's purchased six men-of-war from the Low Countries? And appointed the Marquis de Créqui to command them, and put the Admiral of the Navy in his pay? Do not rule out the thesis that he might constitute a military threat.

Anne But Belle-Isle is strategically important!

Colbert It's not *that* important! He has built a private empire, and set himself above the law!

Anne That is a lie. Monsieur Fouquet is very much admired in society. His only empire is the empire of his friends, of whom I count myself one.

Colbert He has a brother made Archbishop of Narbonne, another Chancellor of the King's Orders, another Grand Squire of the Petite Ecurie, he is bolstered by financiers and fêted by the fashionable élite, he has now got twenty-five armed whaling ships to add to his Dutch destroyers and lines of supply that stretch to Nova Scotia, do you not see how dangerous this is!

Anne You attack him, Monsieur, solely to conceal your own corruption, which this inventory will doubtless bring to light!

Colbert No!

Anne You were the the chief agent of the Cardinal.

Colbert I was his book-man.

Anne Oh, and you gave it all to charity, did you? Didn't squirrel anything away?

Colbert Squirrelling is not in my lexicon.

Anne What is your language, then?

Colbert I do not like unfinished arithmetic.

Henriette and Louise enter at the far end of the hall. They don't see the others at first.

Henriette I long ago resigned myself to a lifetime of humiliation but I allowed myself to think that it was over! What was he saying to you just now?

Louise I only do as I am bid. His Majesty –

Henriette Sssh!

They see the others. They curtsey to the Queen Mother. Colbert bows.

(*to Louise*) Go in.

Louise passes through and exits.

Anne Save me from this prattling bureaucrat. He disparages Monsieur Fouquet.

Henriette Oh, we like Monsieur Fouquet. Monsieur Fouquet is witty.

Anne This one is good at sums.

Colbert I have an equation I cannot resolve, Madame. One of the factors is your maid, La Vallière. That was her, if I'm not mistaken?

41

Henriette It was.

Colbert She is pretty. Oh, indeed.

Anne Of what interest is she to you?

Henriette And the other factor?

Colbert The other factor is the King.

Anne and Henriette exchange a sly smile.

There are rumours. It is a delicate subject, but –

Anne We know all about it, Colbert. You've gone off half-cocked, I'm afraid.

Henriette He looks like he often does that.

Anne We know all about it, Monsieur. A torrid *affaire*, so they say. Blurt it abroad in your Exchequer, to all the whey-faced clerks. Bark it from the rooftops if you dare.

Colbert It is true? And you are not scandalised?

Henriette So bourgeois, this obsession with fidelity . . .

Anne So cramped, Henriette, don't you think? (*to Colbert*) Every woman at court would be honoured to be the King's mistress. Every single one!

Colbert I have a lot of, er, sums to do. Excuse me.

Colbert bows and exits. Pause.

Anne It is working, then?

Henriette Oh yes, I think it is.

Anne and Henriette exit, Henriette maintaining a butter-wouldn't-melt look.

SCENE TEN

The Louvre. The King's table is laid, with one place only, for dinner. There are no forks, only knives. Decanters of wine and water and glasses. The King's chair is brought in. Fouquet enters, with a sheaf of documents. He bows formally to the King's place, and removes his hat. Colbert enters, also carrying documents, bows to the King's place, and removes his hat. Then he bows to Fouquet. They both remain standing.

Colbert Good evening.

Fouquet Good evening.

Colbert How are you?

Fouquet I am tired. Negotiating with tax-men all day.

Colbert Will we soon have agreement?

Fouquet Yes. Soon. (*Pause.*) The King does not dine?

Colbert Entertaining a female, I'm told.

Fouquet Got a scent and gone truffling, eh? Nose in the adulterous mulch? Fine fellow! (*He helps himself to a glass of the King's wine.*) I'd've done the same at that age, when a hand on my knee was sufficient to arouse me, unlike the complex system of weights and pulleys we have to rig up now. God I despise getting old . . .! No one told us fornication was going to require quite so much engineering, did they, Jean-Baptiste?

Colbert (*disapproving*) I am a family man.

Fouquet Why, so am I.

Colbert I like my routines.

Fouquet I too. I make it a rule, if I'm not in bed by two a.m., to go directly home. Who is this temptress who has our sovereign ensnared?

Colbert Her name is La Vallière. Purportedly a maid of honour to Madame.

Fouquet (*aside*) Isn't it galling when the melancholy bites? All going stunningly one minute, your head in a pig's arse the next. – How are your children?

Colbert They prosper. The sons are groomed for high office, the daughters prepared for marriage; they are in sound health and should easily breed. We must increase the population, create the dynasties of the future. Had I power, I would exempt from tax all those who marry young and re-populate France. As for the clergy, they will suffer for their idiotic celibacy.

Fouquet You chide me for my ambitions. You seem to have plenty of your own.

Colbert I don't think I chide you, Superintendent.

Fouquet I don't think you want me to succeed.

Colbert I don't think I remember saying that.

Fouquet But you envy me my triumphs.

Colbert Not at all. I was not made for triumphs. I was made to slowly graft. I'm but a wheel in the grinding-room of government. (*Pause.*) It doesn't look as if we shall be examining accounts tonight, does it? Perhaps soon he will return to the more, er, customary pursuits – hunting, feasting, annexing bits of Belgium – sorry, sorry, I just *cannot* be witty – and leave us to get on with the job . . .?

Fouquet I don't share your optimism.

Colbert I understand. He has caused you a grievous headache with this audit. And he has yet to appoint you First Minister – a post rightfully yours. I should imagine you are not best pleased.

Fouquet I am told that my candidacy is not in question.

Colbert I should certainly hope that it isn't.

Fouquet Doesn't mean I've got it, though, does it?

Colbert He will make the right appointment. In time.

Fouquet Jean-Baptiste . . .

Colbert Yes?

Fouquet I am frightened.

Colbert None of your business is *really* illicit, is it?

Fouquet No. The tariffs and commissions are legitimate. Just some of the book-keeping that's bogus. But my spies say I should be vigilant . . . moves against me are afoot . . . Have you heard anything?

Colbert No, nothing.

Fouquet Tell the truth, for God's sake. Is it you? Are you plotting against me?

Colbert I am not plotting, Superintendent.

Fouquet Can I trust you?

Colbert Can anyone trust anyone?

Fouquet A *friend* would say what he knows.

Colbert Well . . . That fortress you've built is attracting some attention.

Fouquet But why? Belle-Isle guards Quiberon from the Atlantic! Half the Fleet is sheltered there!

Colbert The court knows that you have assembled a fleet of your own. Queen Anne is, if I may paraphrase, well, suspicious. She wonders if you mean the state some harm, what with the boats, and the, er – the artillery isn't going down too well, to be frank.

Fouquet This is a ridiculous accusation.

Colbert She knows that you fell out with Mazarin.

Fouquet How?

Colbert They were close. Some say they were intimate.

Fouquet I'd keep that to yourself if I were you.

Colbert She's aware of the Saint-Mandé project: your plans to retreat to the West.

Fouquet Mazarin plotted to murder me! We quarrelled over a debt, all of a sudden I'm branded a renegade! The second I paid I was back in the fold, my shit shining like a tiara!

Colbert Still, you drafted plans.

Fouquet Oh, I drafted plans – everyone drafts plans! God drafts fucking plans! I've done nothing wrong! I thought the Queen Mother liked me . . .!

Colbert They all like you.

Fouquet No, they just pretend to.

Colbert I find that the ultimate vanity.

Fouquet Oh, it will blow over, no doubt. I just feel defeated today, like a beast of the field, heavy, sodden, with manure slubbed on my fetlocks, I feel inelegant and artless, and nothing has value at all.

Colbert Everything has value.

Fouquet Not when I feel like this.

   Pause.

Colbert Your, er, improvements in the country? How do they progress?

Fouquet I have eighteen thousand people on site. The

house is roofed at last; we near a conclusion. You must
see it. (*brightening*) You must see the garden! I have
creatures of myth cut from porphyry and marble, avenues
of trees which arrive overnight – *orange* trees! – and the
canal! We knocked down three villages to build it! You
can sail, as if on the high seas! Monsieur Le Notre,
geometrist, plans the landscape; Monsier Le Vau, the
château; Monsieur Le Brun, the tapestries and ceilings.
I have a rotunda, several storeys high, over an oval salon,
the floor of which echoes the scheme of the cosmos!

Colbert Your living room represents the cosmos?

Fouquet Yes! It's a work of remarkable originality! You
must see it!

Colbert Dare I hope one day I shall?

Fouquet And of this *nothing*, not a lick of paint, not
the leaf of a lily on the flat of a pond, is arriveable at
without money. I exist to draw money to my side. I love
knowing that if something exists on the planet, money –
my money – can buy it. (*He bows low to the King's place.*)

Colbert You are leaving?

Fouquet Yes. I must make drawings, I have plans for
fountains, hundreds of fountains! I feel sure he (*the King*)
will adore them!

> *Fouquet puts on his hat and leaves. Colbert waits till
> he is gone, then makes a note in pencil in his ledger.
> Then he bows to the King's place, puts on his hat, and
> leaves.*

The gardens of Fontainebleau. Night. Torches. An
orchestra plays. Louise sits on a grassy bank, with a posy
of flowers. She watches as Louis enters dancing.
He performs a ballet called 'Impatience'. He wears a
short flounced skirt which shows off his shapely calves,
and he leaps and capers with skill and verve. He directs
his performance solely to Louise, who laughs gaily and
applauds his more complicated figures. A boys' choir
sings, off.

Choir
    'Sommes-nous pas trop heureux,
    Belle Iris, que vous en semble?
    Nous voici tous deux ensemble,
    Et nous nous parlons nous deux;
    La nuit de ses sombres voiles
    Comme nos désirs ardents,
    Et l'amour et les étoiles
    Et nos secrets confidents . . .'

Louis' dance comes to an end. He bows to Louise,
who is clapping enthusiastically. He flops down next to
her on the grass.

Louise You are manly, oh, so manly! I didn't know you
could dance!

Louis There is much you don't know. You don't, for
instance, know the disposition of my armies, nor my
plans for restructuring the Treasury, nor how keenly, how
hotly I desire you.

Louise (*laughs*) I do! I'm not daft you know!

Louis Oh, you're not?

Louise No!

Louis What should I do with the Treasury, then?

Louise Make it better, of course!

Louis That's the plan. But it's tricky.

Louise You should take charge, because you're the best.

Louis How do you know I'm the best?

Louise Because you're the King, you're the best at everything.

Louis Entrusted by God . . .

Louise Why is it tricky?

Louis The man is my friend. I don't know if he's deceiving me or not.

Louise Well, if he's your friend, he won't be deceiving you, will he?

Louis True.

Louise If you're sure he is your friend . . .

Louis I am sure. Yes, I am.

Louise Choose your friends carefully, and stand by them. That's my father's motto.

Louis It's a good one.

Louise No one betrays a friend.

Louis When I'm with you, the world seems a better place . . . Louise . . .

Louise What was the name of the ballet?

Louis 'Impatience.' I had it composed for you.

Louise (*amazed*) You didn't!

Louis I did. I employ an Italian called Lully. Drinks too much. For a tiny bag of silver he'll write any tune you like.

49

Louise (*laughing*) What kind of tune did you ask for?

Louis leans in and whispers in her ear. Louise's eyes widen.

Hmm. I wonder if it will work . . . ?

Louis We will see.

He kisses her. She responds warmly. He gets his hands inside her clothing very fast.

Louise Stop a minute, stop, stop, please!

Louis sits up, ready to be disappointed.

I only want to say this. I expect nothing. I want no favours, no advantage. I will stand at the back and not know you. If I have babies I will bear them in silence, a long way away.

Louis (*pleased*) You are considerate.

Louise I don't want you to think I have motives for this, I haven't any motives at all, I want nothing, just you. Just . . . you. But I have one question.

Louis Say it.

Louise What shall I call you when you lie in my bed?

They kiss hard. He pulls at her clothes. She grabs at him.

Louis (*whispers in her ear*) Louis. Call me Louis.

He rolls on top of her and hoists up her skirts. He pushes his knee into her crutch, and she moans.

Louise Louis . . . !

End of Act One.

Act Two

SCENE TWELVE

The Louvre. Anne plays cards with Philippe. They play for money.

Philippe I'll raise you five thousand.

Anne Have you got five thousand?

Philippe (*aggrieved*) I have, yes.

They play. Anne wins the hand.

Anne I would like to play *hombre*. But one needs three. Where is Madame?

Philippe She has a rendezvous tonight, with my friend the Comte de Guiche.

Anne I beg your pardon?

Philippe She is sleeping with the Comte de Guiche. She told me.

Anne . . . Are you not angry?

Philippe Most certainly am. I'll kill the little tart when I catch him.

Anne I mean with your wife.

Philippe I'd like to see her whipped round Saint-Germain behind a tumbril. I'd like to have her flambéed as a witch. But a woman must amuse herself somehow, I suppose. The King has dropped her, after all.

Anne Dropped her . . . ?

Philippe Yes, he's in love with that artless girl, what's her name? The dairy-maid. So my wife takes her revenge with my intimates. It is absolutely not to be borne.

Anne He was not supposed to fall for her . . . not the maid . . .!

Philippe Well, he has. He's besotted. He kneels at the foot of her milking-stool, picking straw from between her toes. (*He laughs.*)

Anne He will drive me mad!

> *Fouquet is admitted. His clothes are resplendent. He bows low. Anne recovers her composure and offers her hand for him to kiss. Fouquet advances, kneels, and kisses it.*

Fouquet Majesty, go I to my grave tonight, I die blessed by the touch of your Majesty's hand, my chiefest luxury on earth.

Philippe You are rather good at that, aren't you?

Fouquet The language of a loyal heart, Monsieur, springs to the lips unaided, a jet, a fountain, a cascade of fealty and obeisance.

Philippe Oh, bravo. (*to Anne*) I couldn't do it in a million years.

Fouquet I thought it time that I paid my respects.

Anne One was beginning to wonder. Where have you been all these weeks?

Fouquet I stayed away from the Louvre. I was told your Majesty was displeased.

Anne Displeased?

Fouquet Yes.

Anne With you?

Fouquet With me.

Anne Why?

Fouquet I don't know. But let us just say I was told it.

Anne By whom?

Fouquet No one of importance.

Anne What have you done to incur my displeasure?

Fouquet To the best of my knowledge – nothing.

Anne Then why do you hide? If you have no guilt?

Fouquet I am disposed to calamity. I tend to fear the worst.

Philippe I thought you had a sunny disposition, Superintendent . . .?

Fouquet My sky is clouded by uncertainty, the rain hammers down in my head, I'm not sleeping terribly well.

Anne Hardly the regime of an innocent.

Fouquet Look, I simply invested in the fishing industry, down in my part of the world!

Anne What are you talking about?

Fouquet . . . What are *you* talking about?

Anne I am talking about the state accounts.

Fouquet Oh, the accounts!

Anne My son thinks there may be a problem.

Fouquet Majesty, there isn't a problem!

Anne considers him carefully.

Anne Be at ease. I am heard to say, 'Monsieur Fouquet is my friend.' Am I not heard to say that?

Philippe nods.

Fouquet (*bowing*) My grateful thanks.

Anne We rely on you.

Fouquet Quite. You have a mental picture, I expect, of the thumbscrews I apply to our wretched flock of tax-farmers, in hope of some small stream of revenue actually reaching the Exchequer, rather than branching into the numberless tributaries of greed and graft and perquisite that make up what we laughably call local government. You see in your mind's eye the obloquy that would result were the funds not forthcoming for forays abroad. You visualise the havoc within and without should I suddenly call in my debts – which I might remind you loiter in the region of five million livres – but let's let that pass, it's a trifle.

Anne and Philippe exchange a look of alarm.

I devote myself to you, for years I have devoted myself to your family, to your cause, the best years of my life I might add, and what does the King do? Overlooks me. But, but . . . let's be positive. It is to be wished that his dalliance with this maid of Madame's will remind him that the true purpose of kingship is pleasure, unalloyed pleasure, and that he may asphyxiate in pleasure, suffocate in flesh, drown in youthful delight, and all the world will wish him well, and honour him.

Anne What maid of Madame's?

Fouquet La Vallière.

Anne That is a front.

Fouquet Oh, is it?

Anne A cover for a secret romance, an impossible romance.

Fouquet With whom?

Anne Someone else.

Fouquet Of rank?

Anne (*nods*) And married.

Fouquet Not married to, er . . . (*He discreetly indicztes Phillipe.*)

Anne No! That is over!

Fouquet And the King has seduced no rustic virgins?

Anne None.

Fouquet Ah. (*smiling*) My advice to you is this: encourage His Majesty's deceptions, let him loose on the noblewomen of France, press him to give over this grandiose idea of governing alone, and let us revert to more conventional ways of doing business. To the old ways, the trusted ways, the praxis of the Cardinal. I know how close you were to him. I know your intercourse was . . . fervent. Let us honour his memory, and retrench. This neoteric niggling is no good at all. Thank you for the bountiful gift of your time, Majesty.

Fouquet bows to the Queen.

Philippe I envy your cape.

Fouquet Monsieur?

Philippe Your cape. It's exquisite. Where did you get it?

Fouquet immediately takes off his cape and hands it to Philippe with a flourish. Anne, meanwhile, has a look of thunder.

Fouquet It is yours, Monsieur. (*Fouquet bows low and leaves.*)

Philippe Oh, how lovely! Do you see what he gave me, Mother?

Anne Yes.

55

Philippe A handsome man, Fouquet.

Anne An arrogant man. An overstepping man! A man who gives advice – and born a commoner! – to a Queen of the Bourbon blood!

Philippe Well meant, I'm sure.

Anne Oh, you like the cut of his cloth, the reek of his scent – you fail to see the insolence they mask! He steps in like a tamer to his leopards and his lions, hand on the curb, sweetmeats in the pocket! And claims we owe him money!

Philippe Louis likes him.

Anne I will speak to Louis. (*picking up her cards*) Let's play. What do you wager?

Philippe I'm not playing you, Mother. I always lose.

Anne throws down her cards in annoyance and exits. Philippe examines his new cape closely. He holds the fabric to his cheek, and sighs.

SCENE THIRTEEN

The Louvre. Louis is with Colbert. They examine sheaves of papers.

Louis The Treasury maintain it's legitimate. They call it 'creative accounting'.

Colbert They are bluffing. Fouquet hopes you will not delve too deep.

Louis Are you creative, Colbert?

Colbert In mathematics there can only be one answer. It either adds up, or it doesn't. I fail to see where creativity comes in. That is for painters and poets.

Louis You don't care for painters and poets?

Colbert They have their uses. I envisage a system of patronage, whereby pensions will be paid to those who employ their talents in celebration of your royal strengths and virtues. And not to, er, others. Art is too important to be left to individuals. I would start some sort of academy.

Louis I like that. Good idea.

Colbert I would also proceed against the Superintendent of Finance.

Louis Your allegations are unsupported. It is your word against his.

Colbert Then you must tip the balance.

Louis I could tip it either way.

Colbert You asked before if I was certain. Well, I am. He defrauds the public purse.

Louis I have heard you.

Colbert What then will you do?

Louis I will put it to him.

Colbert He is skilled at debate.

Louis The imputation being that I am not.

Colbert Please, Majesty, let us go through these columns together – red ink, black ink, you see? – look, there are discrepancies here . . . and here . . . and here . . .

Louis I will put it to him.

Colbert The books are cooked! The man is fleecing you!

Louis We will see.

    Philippe enters and bows to Louis.

Philippe You sent for me?

Louis Come in, my dear brother, join us. You know Monsieur Colbert?

Colbert bows low to Philippe.

Philippe Is this where you do the actual business of government and all that sort of thing?

Louis Yes, it is.

Philippe Are we hatching plots and stratagems?

Louis (*smiles*) Be patient for a moment. I have an idea for you. (*to Colbert*) Are we done?

Colbert I have prepared a report. (*He hands it over.*)

Louis (*scanning it*) Your name is not attached.

Colbert I didn't think that, er, that would be appropriate.

Louis And this is sufficient to prosecute?

Colbert Prosecute?

Louis In a court of law.

Colbert . . . I assumed you would just dispose of the problem. Somewhere on the outskirts of the city.

Louis No. It must be seen to be lawful. *If* there is a case.

Colbert I might have to finesse it a little. And of course it might still go against us.

Louis How might it?

Colbert The Superintendent's influence is formidable. He scatters gold like cabbage-seed.

Louis Well, I admire him, he burns like a beacon, he lives like a man ablaze.

Philippe Awfully stylish chap, Fouquet.

Colbert Majesty, he will outshine you, if you let him. The sheen of the patricians must be dulled. You must be the one star in the sky.

Philippe Has he done something wrong?

Louis Philippe, Philippe, let it not concern you. These are economic matters.

Philippe He gave me a rather splendid present.

Colbert He is known for his generosity, Monsieur. But how exactly does he afford it?

Louis Leave us.

Colbert bows and leaves.

Philippe It all sounds horribly complicated.

Louis It is. I am cross with your wife.

Philippe (*sighs*) I don't know which is worse, politics or marriage. I can't keep up with any of it.

Louis She has started an *affaire* with the Comte de Guiche.

Philippe Yes.

Louis They flaunt their lust in public.

Philippe nods unhappily.

I take it as an insult.

Philippe How do you think I take it?

Louis He is not even royal.

Philippe You should see the size of him, though. Phew!

Louis They do not respect me, Philippe. I lack the potency to command their absolute obedience. I want you to aid me with this.

Philippe I'd love to help, but I'm useless, really.

Louis There is one field in which your gifts surpass those of my legislators.

Philippe There is?

Louis The first code of etiquette was drawn up in 1585. Since then it has been often revised, but the changes are piecemeal. I want a comprehensive overhaul. I want a new style of etiquette at court, an accurate table of precedence, a minutely detailed schedule of who does what, when, how – a systematic code of conduct which will apply to all. Everyone!

Philippe Oh, quite.

Louis The grandees think they have an automatic claim to a share in political power. They do not.

Philippe Yes, protocol is vital. One must know where to stand, when to sit, which goblet to use, how to address an ambassador's sister, all of that. Do you know, I do reckon standards have slipped.

Louis Not yours. Your bearing is impeccable at all times.

Philippe How very civil of you.

Louis Could you do this for me? Could you notate the rules and regulations for daily life at court? With emphasis on the minutiae of rank?

Philippe Well, I'll have a shot at it.

Louis Bless you. (*He hugs him.*)

Philippe I am very sorry for the errors of Madame.

Louis Don't mention it. Not your fault the mare is on heat. But the affront is sharp. Make her pay.

Anne enters. They bow to her.

Louis Mother.

Philippe Mother.

Anne (*to Philippe*) What are *you* doing here?

Louis We have been having a conversation.

Anne Bring it to an end.

Louis Thank you for your help, Philippe.

Philippe Pleasure. Goodnight, Mother. (*Philippe kisses Anne's hand and turns to leave. He turns back.*) Do you know, I'm really rather fond of Monsieur Fouquet. I'd hate to see anything happen to him.

Louis (*smiles*) I am fond of him too.

   Philippe exits, reassured.

Anne I also am fond. But that is irrelevant. I do not talk to clerks. But Colbert came to me. He claims irregularities at the Exchequer. He claims a naval build-up in the west.

Louis What do you mean?

Anne I mean Fouquet has amassed a private army. The security of the state is at risk. The security of the family! You may not hazard your family! On top of that, he has had the gall to give me advice. How do we get through to these people that they will give their advice *when we ask for it*? – And he said we are in his debt. He said five million livres. He said he wants it back.

Louis . . . Go on.

Anne He thinks he is mightier than us. He thinks we are his puppets. The conceit!

Louis I have investigated his department. The picture isn't clear; there may be some underhand dealing. There may be some grounds for action.

Anne Well, act. Before he does.

Louis But I like the man!

Anne Kill him.

Louis And make us look like butchers? And spark a civil war? I am trying to create a modern state, a politics of consensus – yes, a new way – and you want to plunge us back to the days of outrage and massacre?

Anne Very well. Arrest him. Try him. Then kill him.

Louis I thought you were fond of him!

Anne Not any more.

Louis God, you're cold!

Anne We cannot have this peacock-tail of condescension fanned before our eyes! We must preserve the seniority of blood!

Louis . . . What has he done? Actually?

Anne He gave offence. He dishonoured the name of the Cardinal. That, I cannot tolerate. Don't you see, I am trying to protect you!

Louis I do not need protecting!

Anne You do, my darling. You let yourself be influenced by little slips of girls.

Louis I'm in love, Mother.

Anne In love?

Louis Yes, and loved in return.

Anne Rubbish.

Louis It's true!

Anne La Vallière is a whore and a conspirator.

Louis Mother, she is virtuous!

Anne No woman is virtuous. Discard her.

Pause. They eye each other. Louis comes to a decision.

Louis I am not prepared to do as you say.

Anne Louis!

Louis I trust my judgement. Louise is good. I am loved as a lover, not just as a king. This is a novel experience and actually very nice, and I'm not giving it up.

Anne Do you dare go against me?

Louis Yes. You're no longer Regent. And my will is stronger than yours.

Pause. Anne considers.

Anne Give me Fouquet, then.

Louis But he's my friend!

Anne Give me Fouquet, and keep the girl. Put aside your finer feelings, and strike for your family, your ancestry, your throne. We're not paying him five million livres. He can whistle for it.

SCENE FOURTEEN

The gardens of the Tuileries. Louise walks through with a basket of flowers, humming a country song. Fouquet suddenly appears from behind a statue.

Fouquet Mademoiselle . . .

Louise (*alarmed*) Monsieur Fouquet?

Fouquet (*glancing around*) Let us come straight to the meat. (*He holds up a purse.*) Two hundred thousand livres in *louis* of gold.

Louise Why?

Fouquet Why? Because your skin is a pigment as yet uninvented, your eyes incandesce like distant stars, your hair is a weave of angels' wings, your lips are like . . . your lips are like . . . (*aside*) Would you believe I've forgotten? It is the curse of growing old, a most lamentable evaporation of memory. – This (*the purse*) is for a rendezvous of one evening, no more. In my house at Saint-Mandé.

Louise Monsieur, have you hair growing out of your shoulders, like my father?

Fouquet In the raw, I look near prehistoric. And my fur is all my own.

Louise shivers with distaste.

Louise Thank you, I think I shall decline.

Fouquet It is a mark of virility!

She turns to leave. Fouquet comes after her.

Mademoiselle, I beg you, reconsider. I have so much to give! Come to me for one night, luxuriate in licentious-ness, my wife is away in the country. I have influence, taste, refinement, I lay on extravagant surprises. I can make your life glitter with possibility!

Louise Why me?

Fouquet Because you have me in your power! I am sick with love for you!

Louise I love another.

Fouquet You are too young to know who you love.

Louise No, I'm not! And what I give him can't be bought! You gentlemen of the court think everything's for sale, don't you? It's a horrible way to live, and to be frank, I find you disgusting. I often wish I had stayed in

64

Touraine! But the man I love has a good, true heart. So there is *some* decency here.

Louise exits. Fouquet sits among the statues, disconsolate.

Fouquet Is it any wonder I get depressed? (*Pause.*) Her provincial notions of virtue. In five years she'll have fucked half of Paris.

Henriette enters and sees him.

Henriette Have you turned to stone?

Fouquet (*grumpily*) No, I was stone, I've turned back to putty. The work of a hundred words . . .

Henriette I saw Louise. Was she with you?

Fouquet I offer her the universe, she prefers the farmyard.

Henriette You propositioned her?

He nods.

What made you think you would succeed?

Fouquet Had a rush of blood to the loins. It's very interesting the way the arteries work. This fellow I sponsor tells me that –

Henriette You know she is sleeping with the King?

Fouquet No she isn't, that is a camouflage they've concocted, to disguise his lust for some high-born bint, who is kept in cryptic concealment.

Henriette That was me.

Fouquet Madame . . .?

Henriette I was the high-born bint.

Fouquet . . . I regret my gross lapse into the vernacular. When glum I kiss goodbye to my usual oratorical gifts. And I congratulate you, Madame. It must be deemed a superlative catch.

Henriette No, no, it's finished, he threw me over. For her. He fell in love with her.

Fouquet Her?

Henriette Louise. You see? The scheme didn't work. She really is sleeping with the King.

Fouquet Holy fucking God and all His shitty little Angels.

Henriette It's not a day for oratory, is it?

Fouquet I have just insulted the King's mistress. (*Thinks.*) *You* must speak for me! You have his ear. (*Gives her the purse.*) Take this, it is yours, take it, just tell him it was all a mistake! At the first opportunity, tell him! I thought she was someone else! I was drunk, I was mad, I was playing a joke!

Henriette He is my enemy now.

Fouquet No, no, he can't be!

Henriette I offended him. He goads the court to hurt me. If I were you I would saddle your fastest horse. Run to the country, tend your estates, hope in some years you'll be pardoned.

Fouquet I can't do that! I'm about to be made First Minister!

Henriette A singular event occurred last Friday. I had a conversation with my husband. He tells me he was in the presence of the King when details of your ruin were discussed. I don't think you're about to be made First Minister. I think you're abouit to be killed! Flee, Monsieur! Flee while you have the chance!

Pause. Fouquet digests this.

Fouquet Ruin? I am not familiar with this term.

Henriette They are plotting against you, Monsieur!

Fouquet But the King is my friend. Apart from inadvertently angling to get between the legs of his pubescent courtesan, I have done nothing wrong. I had a bad night, that's all. My wife is away, I was . . . lonely. I got up this morning and bethought myself the boy I used to be. We all have our failings, Madame.

Henriette We do.

Fouquet I'm in thrall to my diminishing libido. What a very sad sight I must be.

Henriette (*taking his hand*) There is still time. Make your escape, I beg you.

Fouquet . . . Would you come with me?

Henriette . . . Come with you where?

Fouquet To Belle-Isle? I have a little navy, we'll be safe.

Henriette I can't come with you to Belle-Isle. You know that.

Fouquet But would you if you could?

Henriette I would give it serious consideration.

Fouquet That's the nicest thing anyone's said to me for weeks. I'm not finished, you know.

Henriette I hope you're not.

Fouquet I'm not. You found me wandering distracted through the gardens of the Tuileries, and you concluded that I'd lost my grip. But nothing could be further from what we euphemistically call the truth. – I'll have my money back, thank you.

Henriette smiles, fondly but sadly, and hands back the purse.

It will all be fine.

He kisses her hand. They exit in different directions.

SCENE FIFTEEN

The Louvre. Louis and Louise.

Louis I will string his guts for rigging on the flagship of my fleet! I will flay his skin for spinnakers, his balls can test the wind! The presumption of the man! He didn't – harm you in any way?

Louise No, he was courteous.

Louis Yes, he dresses it in courtesy, his impertinence, his disdain!

Louise I simply told him that I love another. You.

Louis Did you say me?

Louise I didn't think I ought.

Louis But everybody knows. How could he not know?

Louise He didn't seem to.

Louis He must have!

Louise I don't think it is so important, Louis.

Louis What you think is incidental! (*He immediately regrets this.*) I'm sorry, my love, please excuse my temper. You are so much more than I deserve. How was I so lucky as to stumble upon you?

Louise You were chasing someone else, as I recall.

Louis (*laughs*) It's true. But all that is over now. I will never stray from your side, Louise.

Louise You will be with me for as long as you are with me. I don't complain.

Louis You don't complain, do you? I think you're the only one in the kingdom who doesn't . . .

They kiss. Louis gets aroused.

Louise We can't. Not here.

He is forced to agree, and backs off.

Louis I want to take you somewhere. Where we can be alone. My father had a hunting-box in a village called Versailles. It's nothing special, no one ever goes there. I am thinking I shall have it modified for you.

Louise For me?

Louis The country round about, well, it's boggy and swampy, but that won't affect us, as we'll never get out of bed.

Louise You treat me like a princess.

Louis I treat you a lot better than that.

They kiss again. They can't resist each other.

Go now. You must go. I have a meeting. Dream about Versailles.

Louise I'll dream about the bed, and you in it.

They kiss hotly, then Louise tears herself away, and exits. Louis straightens his wig. He rings a bell. Colbert is admitted. He bows.

Louis Is Fouquet waiting?

Colbert nods.

I will see if he makes some admission of guilt. Then I want him arrested. Have the Captain of the Guard standing by. Pick him up as he tries to leave the palace.

Colbert I'm afraid that, er, won't be possible, Majesty.

Louis What?

Colbert It would be a tactical error.

Louis He sneers at me! I want him thrown in gaol!

Colbert There are a number of obstacles to such an initiative. Which is why I had foreseen us going down the other route.

Louis What other route?

Colbert The ditch, the daggers –

Louis No. What are the obstacles?

Colbert First, the collection of taxes for this year.

Louis I thought you said the tax-farmers were corrupt?

Colbert Yes, but we do need the money. The Superintendent is presently negotiating with these, er, persons. It would for obvious reasons be advantageous to have this deal concluded prior to arraigning him for trial. Or next year we shall all have nothing to eat. Second, your Majesty may have temporarily forgotten that Monsieur Fouquet is Attorney-General to the Parliament of Paris. He therefore has a right to elect to be tried by his peers, that is, the, er, Parliament. Which is loosely the same as electing to be tried by your best friends and several close relations. It is unlikely that we would want this. Finally, an arrest will require meticulous planning. Should anything go wrong – should he have a chance to flee to Brittany – should he gain his redoubt at Belle-Isle – we are looking at civil unrest.

Louis You're telling me I have to let him alone?

Colbert For the time being. And you have to persuade him to resign the Attorney-Generalship.

Louis How do I do that?

Colbert Majesty, you wished to practise statecraft; this will test your skill.

Louis . . . Send him in.

Colbert exits. Louis composes himself. A moment later Fouquet enters. He bows low.

Fouquet Majesty, in all the days of my nugatory life, never have I –

Louis Don't flatter me, Fouquet.

Fouquet It is a legend carved in stone that your Majesty's –

Louis Just stop it.

Fouquet is silent.

We once played a game of billiards, do you remember? You were kind enough to let me win.

Fouquet I lost fair and square, Majesty.

Louis I love billiards. But no one will give me a decent match. Do you want to play again?

Fouquet Not, perhaps, tonight.

Louis No, we have to discuss these accounts.

Fouquet Everything is shipshape, I hope?

Louis . . . Not quite one hundred per cent.

Fouquet . . . You are making me nervous.

Louis Please, don't be nervous. I am mindful of the service you've performed the crown. My mother has brought certain things to my attention, certain actions on your part that shall we say abetted my continuance on this throne?

71

Fouquet I tried to help. I had little sympathy for the rebels of the Fronde.

Louis Because . . .?

Fouquet Because society would have broken down, the mechanisms of business would have warped and fragmented, there would have been no structure, no markets, no trade.

Louis No chance to turn a profit?

Fouquet The globe revolves on profit. Profit presupposes growth. Without growth, we go backwards. If we are rich, France is rich.

Louis But I am not rich.

Fouquet Let us just say you are temporarily embarrassed. It will change. Trust me.

Louis That is what I want to hear, my friend! Do you think I can amass a great fortune, for myself, for my heirs?

Fouquet Without question.

Louis (*consulting documents*) Conceivably by purchasing old, unredeemed bills on the Treasury, at say three or four per-cent of their nominal value, and then re-assigning them against solvent funds, different budgets under different headings, and getting them repaid in full?
As you have done?

Fouquet (*smiles*) We call it re-scheduling a debt, Majesty. It is common practice.

Louis Some call it sharp practice.

Fouquet The air is thick with comedians. That Molière. What a monkey!

Louis Nevertheless, my assistants inform me that there are inadequacies in this audit.

Fouquet Who are your assistants?

Louis Little elves in the woods.

Fouquet Who know as much of finance as they know of – what? – billiards?

Louis Actually I use them for the balls.

Fouquet laughs.

Are you telling me you can justify this debt of five million livres which it's claimed is owed to you?

Fouquet Of course I can. Do you want to see receipts?

Louis Receipts? What are your receipts worth?

Fouquet Five million livres.

Louis You deny there is any malpractice?

Fouquet There is none whatsoever. I suspect your elves to be deficient at addition and subtraction. High finance is a sophisticated art.

Louis I would prefer to consider it a science.

Fouquet I would prefer you don't consider it at all. That is what I am here for.

Louis I would prefer you forbore from telling me how to do my job, Superintendent.

Fouquet bows.

I *will* have a say in this. There is nothing more shameful than to be king in title only.

Fouquet And yet, and yet, there must be constraints.

Louis Why? Don't you trust me?

Fouquet You are the chief administrator – but not, I must insist, the owner – of the body politic.

Louis I am the state.

Fouquet It may be that the state resides symbolically in your person, but you are not free to run it entirely as you wish. You will grant me that point, I hope.

Louis I am not free to run my own person? What if I want a shit?

Fouquet There is a system of checks and balances, brought into being for good reasons. Government is not your responsibility alone.

Louis (*fiercely*) Oh yes it is. (*Pause.*) You voice the view of Parliament. But God who has given kings to men wished them to be respected as His lieutenants, reserving to Himself the right to examine their conduct. Here is a fundamental principle: you agree that you hold certain privileges, certain rights?

    Fouquet nods.

You do so purely from my liberality. At a stroke I can take them away. On a whim, Monsieur, if I choose. Dash them to the ground.

Fouquet The English King was of similar opinions. Till his subjects lopped off his head.

Louis But this is France. We have no savage republicans here. And I do not much like your tone.

Fouquet Oh, my tone will be the death of me. I am prone to gabble persiflage I do not really mean.

Louis I am prone to issue warrants when the joke's at my expense.

    Fouquet looks unnerved. Louis claps him on the back.

I'm having fun with you, man! We'll agree to differ on the matter of my prerogatives. And I'll do my best to keep my head. And if you tell me that the books are in order, why then, the books are in order. Meanwhile I have a proposition for you. Séguier, the Chancellor, is as you know old and infirm. He should be replaced. I am thinking that you might replace him.

Fouquet I am honoured.

Louis I remain undecided about my First Minister, but that would obviously be a step towards – ah, but I'm forgetting something! It is not legal for the same man to hold both the office of Chancellor and that of Attorney-General to the Parliament of Paris. Who invented these stupid rules?

Fouquet Parliament, I'm afraid. It's to prevent the consolidation of too much power within the sphere of one individual.

Louis Well, I'm sure that's absolutely right. You know my views. I leave it with you. How is your love life?

Fouquet My what?

Louis Any luck with the ladies?

Fouquet . . . Has someone said something?

Louis No, no one has said anything. Why, what is wrong?

Fouquet I have on occasion blundered on to private property.

Louis Haven't we all? Who knows what the boundaries are, nowadays?

Fouquet You are having sport with me.

Louis I admit: I'm having fun. Come on, let's talk about women. Can you not give me some guidance? You're a man of many conquests, so I'm told. A giant among whoremongers, a fantastic fucker. What's your secret?

Fouquet I may not be the fucker you suppose.

Louis You have power; females fall upon their knees before you, surely?

Fouquet I do not have quite the power to assure it.

Louis Who does?

Fouquet The royal muscle, I gather, is rampant.

Louis (*laughs*) Nonetheless, I could still use some tips.

Fouquet The thing you must do is be nice to your wife. Happy domesticity's the secret of success. Then you can play the field in peace.

Louis Now that *is* good advice.

Fouquet I hope you will take it, Majesty. Don't waste your youth on paperwork! Devote your days to debauchery! I did when I was young. I was often told I was beautiful; I like to think I was. But, but . . . it goes all too soon. At least I still have my own hair.

Louis And have you a mistress, at present?

Fouquet Too busy, Majesty, too busy. I am tendering for a slice of the West Indies; I have expeditions to Madagascar, Guadeloupe; down in Brittany I'm harvesting sardines.

Louis Good God, do you never stop?

Fouquet I do. I rest. I retire to my place in the country.

Louis This is Vaux-le-Vicomte?

Fouquet It is.

Louis I hear you have made some improvements.

Fouquet I have created, I believe, a paradise. Would you care to visit?

Louis Thank you, I would.

Fouquet A date in August? For the sun?

Louis Let us fix on a fine day in August. I'll bring my family?

Fouquet Delighted.

Louis With luck Monsieur and Madame will behave.

Fouquet The court is ablaze with their discord.

Louis Yes, I do what I can to fan the flames.

Fouquet Is that wise?

Louis It suits me to have them locked in battle. If they're attacking each other, they're not attacking me. You see? I am learning to be cunning.

Fouquet Why are you telling me these confidences, Majesty?

Louis I wouldn't want you to think I was naive.

Fouquet But I don't.

Louis But you do. Now, I needn't keep you any longer.

Fouquet We part as friends, I hope . . . ?

Louis Why ever should we not?

Fouquet Majesty, you have my deep love.

Fouquet bows and exits. Louis is exhausted. He takes off his wig. His head is shaved, patchily; he is going prematurely bald. He steps out of his high-heeled shoes. Without the wig and shoes, he looks smaller. He sits.

Louis (*quietly*) Colbert.

Colbert enters from a side door. He is slightly shocked at the sight that greets him. He has a document.

What's that?

Colbert I have drawn up plans for the execution. When the, er, verdict is returned.

A blast of loud, celebratory music leads us into:

SCENE SIXTEEN

The gardens of Vaux-le-Vicomte on 17 August 1661. Early evening. the music recedes; it now comes from a distant orchestra. There are the sounds of crowds of people. Philippe and Henriette enter, acknowledging admirers on either side.

Henriette Six thousand people! How will he manage it?

Philippe He has outdone himself. Even you would be hard pressed to pleasure six thousand at once.

Henriette I was referring to the banquet. I was referring to meat in our mouths.

Philippe So was I, dear heart.

Henriette Well, I walked into that.

Philippe Keep walking. Good practice for when I sell your carriage.

Henriette You wouldn't!

Philippe One coach is more than enough. I fail to see why we need two.

Henriette We can't fit all your frocks into one.

Philippe Then we'll leave yours behind, as you seem so much happier without them.

Henriette Some men appreciate the female form.

Philippe So? Some men sleep with goats.

Henriette My friend de Guiche says I'm not unlike a sylph of ancient Rome.

Philippe He means you have a nice arse, dear – he's indifferent to what's round the front.

Henriette Well, at least he prefers mine to yours. – Look at those fountains! Aren't they divine?

She has noticed that Anne is approaching, on the arm of Louis. There is muted applause. Louis wears an even bigger wig and higher shoes than previously.

Philippe We walk through walls of water, twice the height of a man . . . It is like the throne of Neptune . . . a lost city under the sea . . .

Henriette I loved the canal! The barques and barges on it!

Philippe I loved the avenue of orange trees. The scent still lingers, damp, exotic. What think you of Vaux-le-Vicomte, Mother?

Anne One is impressed. It is a garden of intelligence.

Philippe It should restore Fouquet to favour, I expect?

Anne One particularly admires the harmony of horizontal planes, the axial composition, culminating there, at the point of convergence of every perspective. Brilliant.

Philippe Yes, I was about to say that.

Anne See the broderies of box on the terraces, Philippe? They look like Turkish carpets.

Philippe Such wit! Such invention! He tries so hard to please.

Henriette (*to Louis*) Do you adore it too?

Louis (*curtly*) Yes.

Henriette leads Louis aside.

79

Henriette The most important people in the country are here.

Louis (*sourly*) Yes, well, it's Monsieur Fouquet, isn't it?

Henriette He is not a bad man, Louis.

Louis Having a nice garden makes you good, does it? . . . I remember what you said at Fontainebleau.

Henriette (*smiles*) I called it a wilderness.

Louis Compared to this, it is.

Henriette How lovely that we're talking. Can we be friends again?

Louis Certainly. But stand your ground against my brother. He makes a drama out of nothing.

Anne The dinner is cooked by the great chef Vatel. I wish it was ready. I'm starved.

Philippe Where are all the guests going to sit?

Anne Well, we shall be indoors, no doubt.

Philippe (*to Louis*) Have you been inside? It's absolutely sumptuous. Tapestries on every wall!

Anne (*looking at the château*) Remarkable sense of scale. Grand, but not too grand. And that extraordinary dome!

> *The orchestra plays a fanfare and the people applaud as Fouquet enters. He is dressed spectacularly, in motifs of the sun. The royals all applaud him. He bows low.*

Fouquet Welcome, Majesty, your Majesty, welcome, Monsieur and Madame, to my little country fête.

Philippe Bravo, Fouquet.

Henriette It's entrancing!

Fouquet It has only just begun. We shall now ascend to the salon, where a light repast will be served. We have some pheasant, some ortolan, some quail, a quantity of partridge, lobster and crab, and wines from every sun-seared hillside in the south. Our glorious sovereign shall be served on plates of gold. Everyone else shall have silver.

Henriette All of them?

Fouquet Every one! Subsequently, if your Majesty permits, we shall adjourn to the grotto, down by the lake, where an entertainment is presented by my pet clown Molière. As it is getting dark, the stage will be –

Louis What are you dressed as, Fouquet?

Fouquet I am dressed as the Sun, Majesty.

Louis Aren't you hot?

Fouquet I am baking, Majesty. I may cause a minor drought.

Louis But why? Why the Sun?

Fouquet Because of the unique quality of its radiance, because of the light it imparts to other stars, because it stimulates activity in every corner of the world, because it's constantly in motion yet seems always tranquil, and all these things I thought this day I might apply to me.

The royals laugh. Louis joins in, grimly.

Louis We thank you for your efforts, Superintendent.

Louis offers his hand for Fouquet to kiss his ring. Fouquet kneels and kisses it.

Fouquet (*softly*) I have sold the office of Attorney-General, Majesty.

Louis Then your motto may come true. Like your squirrel, you may rise and rise.

Fouquet stands, glowing with pleasure.

Fouquet May I invite you all to dinner? I have attempted for your delectation to combine all the arts into one unforgettable experience. I have decided today that I love everything. Everything in the world, I love! And above all else, I love fireworks!

Fouquet gives a signal and a huge display of fireworks commences.

Philippe Bravo!

Fouquet One thousand rockets!

Henriette Oh look! They form fleurs-de-lys!

Philippe (*aside to Henriette*) Perhaps one will land on your head. (*to Fouquet*) Lead on!

Fireworks explode over their heads as Fouquet, Philippe and Henriette exit. Louis lingers with Anne. He smiles throughout, waving to the crowds.

Louis An unforgettable experience. Well, it certainly is.

Anne (*looking at the house*) A most striking piece of modernism.

Louis I thought you disliked progress.

Anne He has the bravado to bring it off.

Louis I want to arrest him *now*.

Anne No! You can't!

Louis He has planned this. It's a deliberate provocation. His friends will look at my dilapidated châteaux, my overgrown gardens, and they will laugh behind their hands! I've a troop of musketeers at the gate. At a signal they could put out this sun.

Anne Louis, you cannot arrest the man at his own party! Too dangerous! Wait until you can do it on your terms, on your territory, not his.

Louis Why not his? You overrate this place, Mother. It's only a house.

Anne The finest in France.

Louis It's too small, surely?

Anne It's architecturally perfect.

Louis But small. Look, he is standing on his terrace, waving to the crowds, like an Emperor in triumph.

Anne Come, I want my dinner.

> *They exit towards the house, through the excited*
> *crowds. Fireworks explode above.*

SCENE SEVENTEEN

Two weeks later. An ante-room in Nantes, Brittany. Colbert waits. A heavy door creaks open, off. Fouquet is pushed into the room. He has his hands tied behind his back and a hood over his head. He stands uncertainly, panting. Colbert walks slowly around him. Fouquet waits, frightened. He can hear Colbert's breath. Colbert leaves the room.

Fouquet I am Nicolas Fouquet.

> *Louis enters. Fouquet can't see him.*

Louis Good morning, Monsieur Fouquet.

Fouquet Majesty.

Louis They did not harm you?

Fouquet I was treated with courtesy.

Louis Good.

Fouquet But could you not have done it more discreetly? Why in a busy market square? And why in Brittany, a day's ride from my castle, right in the midst of my people?

Louis I had to come to Nantes. You had to come to Nantes.

Fouquet Yes, the Estates-General is meeting.

Louis Well, I thought it would be convenient. Besides, it's my birthday.

Fouquet Oh, this is your idea of a treat?

Louis (*smiles*) I am twenty-three. How old are you, Monsieur?

Fouquet Old enough to see death in the distance.

Louis Nicely put. (*Pause.*) I did want your arrest to have a degree of publicity. And I did want to effect it on your home ground, where you feel secure, where your power-base is centred.

Fouquet Because . . . ?

Louis Well, it's straightforward, isn't it? If I can take *you*, *here* – I can take anybody, anywhere.

Fouquet I made a genuine mistake with the girl. Had I known she was yours I would never have approached her.

Louis It has nothing to do with the girl.

Fouquet is alarmed and confused.

Fouquet Then what?

Louis You have been stealing from me.

Fouquet No, I haven't.

Louis You have undermined the state.

Fouquet No!

Louis I have evidence.

Fouquet That's impossible, I don't write anything down!

Louis I have the evidence of my eyes and the evidence of my heart.

Fouquet Easily demolished in front of a jury.

Louis Who said anything about a jury?

Now Fouquet is really worried.

Fouquet I see, it's like that.

Louis Yes, that's how it is.

Louis goes up to Fouquet and yanks off the hood. He sits. Fouquet remains standing.

Fouquet Are you going to kill me?

Louis Probably.

Fouquet But why? I've done nothing wrong!

Louis Because I can. (*Pause.*) I will not be eclipsed, Monsieur. I will not be a cold little meteor beside your blazing sun.

Fouquet Two weeks ago we were the best of friends . . .!

Louis Two weeks ago you humiliated me.

Fouquet I set off a thousand rockets in your honour!

Louis You made me look small. I am the King of France.

Fouquet You could have shared in my prosperity!

Louis I do not want to share in your swindles! (*Pause.*) You showed me the future. I'm grateful. You showed me how a King should live, with taste and refinement, with all the trappings of success. Now I shall take your ideas.

Fouquet Ideas are free. You can have the ideas.

Louis All your properties and all your possessions are confiscate. Your assets are frozen and transferred to the crown. I have sent for your architect, your gardener and the chap who does the tapestries. I will have the plates and the silver and the chairs. I am digging out your orange trees and having them re-planted.

Fouquet Where?

Louis Oh, I'm doing up a property of my own.

Fouquet Not my orange trees . . .!

Louis Everything.

Fouquet So you liked it? Vaux-le-Vicomte?

Louis The poetry of your gardens was exquisite. The victory of rule over disorder.

Fouquet I wanted to impress you.

Louis And the house itself, a marvel.

Fouquet Bravo, Fouquet.

Louis But too small, surely? Too small. I am thinking I'll expand on your model. I'll make the whole affair ten times bigger. Twenty times bigger!

Fouquet Will I ever see it?

Louis No.

Pause.

Fouquet I'm now in a position where I'll say anything at all to save my life.

Louis Ah, the miracle of language.

Fouquet I'm prepared to beg! Don't kill me.

Louis Why not?

Fouquet Because I'm begging you not to!

Louis Is that a good enough reason?

Fouquet Oh, God!

Louis Please, let us talk together like statesmen. All I am going to do is to put you on trial for embezzlement and conspiracy.

Fouquet Thank you, Majesty, thank you.

Louis Don't mention it. The penalty is, of course, death.

Fouquet But I shall fight the case. I have a right to be tried by Parliament.

Louis Ah, no, not any more. You're no longer Attorney-General, are you?

Fouquet . . . That's very clever.

Louis I thought you were the one who was clever.

Fouquet Yes, I thought that, too.

Louis I am thinking I'll appoint a tribunal.

Fouquet Nevertheless, the law is specific – I have a right to defend myself!

Louis Look. You cling to power when your time is past. There is no longer a post of Superintendent of Finance. I abolished it this morning.

Fouquet At least Colbert won't get it.

Louis I have appointed Colbert Controller-General of Finance.

Fouquet I understand what you're doing. But I don't understand why. The system worked! Flawed, yes, like human beings, flawed, fatigued, but it worked! Why do you want to alter it?

Louis Because I can.

Fouquet But nothing will ever change! Not *really*! Men will always be corrupt, men will always be corruptible. Throughout history there's been no real progress. Oh, we have printing machines, we have muskets, but our souls are as black as a medieval sewer.

Louis Yet you build for the future. You break all the rules.

Fouquet Because I want to live well! Because faced with such a stew of mediocrity and graft, the only recipe is to live well, and try and get fucked occasionally!

Louis I'm afraid you'll never get fucked again, Monsieur.

Fouquet I'm afraid of that too. But I'll fight.

Louis I'll win. I am the living law.

Fouquet Such heights of vanity in one so young.

Louis No, there is no vanity, there's only rightful power. My power. I'm sorry. I liked you very much.

Louis stands up to leave.

Fouquet We used to go hunting together!

Louis That was when I was a boy.

Fouquet But why modernise merely for the sake of modernising? Everything will still be the same!

Louis It will not be the same. It will be better.

Fouquet What, with Colbert at the helm? All that will happen is his people will replace mine in every network, every tentacle of vested interest the length and breadth of the land, and we will all have to live in this rational world of the Jean-Baptistes, this method and prudence and nest-eggs and pensions, this world where what counts is the neatness of the files! Holy Christ! What of our gut instincts, our primal sense of how we ought to live? What of our soaring hopes? What of our great adventuring failures and calamities, our discoveries of things we didn't know we were looking for, the marvellous accidents of science? No place for them in Colbert's world; no one sent a memo. Oh, lock me in the Bastille; I'll prefer it.

Louis I will make improvements.

Fouquet No, you won't make improvements. You'll never do anything, because you have no style.

Louis (*quietly furious*) We will see.

Fouquet I don't deserve this!

Louis Look. It may be that you're innocent. It simply doesn't matter.

Louis leaves the room. We hear the heavy door slam, off, and bolts are drawn.

Fouquet I'm not finished, you know!

SCENE EIGHTEEN

Three years later. The gardens of Versailles, which are still under construction. Anne enters with Philippe, Henriette and Colbert.

Anne Three years, Colbert! You've had three years!

Colbert Fouquet's defence was well argued.

Anne Yes, the whole of Paris is familiar with his case!

Colbert He wrote it on strips torn off from his shirt, and smuggled it out of the prison.

Philippe I *thought* his clothes looked a bit tattered.

Henriette I went to court every day. He was ever so dashing.

Anne He's not meant to be dashing, he's meant to be dead! I hate this place! It's all mud and workmen!

Philippe They drop by the hundred from malaria. They take them away in the middle of the night.

Henriette I wish they'd take you away in the middle of the night.

Colbert There he is!

> *Colbert points towards Louis in the distance, and they exit.*
> *Louis enters from another direction with Louise on his arm. He looks older and more distinguished. His clothes are even more ostentatious than previously – his wig bigger, and his shoes higher.*

Louis (*with a map*) It's best to approach this parterre from the east. One should pause momentarily – here – to admire the view, and then go straight to the orangery, from where one will see row upon row of orange trees – twelve hundred and fifty of them! – and the lake that the Swiss Guards are digging.

Louise Oh, let's see it!

Louis I thought I'd write down the optimum route. So none will stray.

Louise Who would stray? It's lovely.

Louis New sculptures arrive every day. My groves and fountains will be populated with amazons and bacchants, tritons and naiads, dozens and dozens of them. We will think ourselves transported to Olympia!

Louise I'm so happy here, Louis.

Anne, Philippe, Henriette and Colbert enter.

Louis I designed it all for you.

Anne (*approaching*) I thought Le Nôtre designed it.

Bows are exchanged. Louise curtsies low to Anne and keeps her head down.

Louis We work together, Mother. He consults me on the flowers. Apparently I'm rather good at colour. So we have brilliancy all the year round!

Anne What, even in winter?

Louis In winter the beds are replanted every day. Nothing will fade at Versailles.

Colbert Majesty, there is news. The tribunal has passed judgement.

Louis Death?

Colbert No.

Louis What do you mean, no?

Colbert Nine votes for death. Thirteen for banishment.

Louis Banishment! After three years of investigation! Can't they hand down the right sentence?

Colbert As I warned you, he has many friends. Due process was observed. It is, er, legal.

Louis I say what is legal! (*to his family*) They have merely banished him!

Anne We know that.

Philippe I must admit I'm a little bit relieved. I hate to see a handsome man dismembered.

Louis But he will plot against us from abroad! He will gather his forces and fight us!

Philippe I think we could show clemency. He has been ever so useful.

Louis But I wanted him dead!

Philippe I say, steady on. The fellow is awfully witty.

Henriette Witty, and weak, and old. (*She takes Louis aside.*) I know this man. He's harmless. He cares about his dignity, his figure in the world. His clothes and his hair and his mastery of language. But he does not covet your throne.

Louis (*calming down*) Go on.

Henriette With his speeches from the dock he made himself the darling of Paris. Nobody wants him dead. A great king would – surely – spare the life of his vanquished enemy. A great King would show himself merciful, and bask in the love of his people. You are a great king, Louis. Live and let live. Please.

Louis Nicely put, Madame. (*He considers.*) Very well. I will spare your friend on one condition: you must end your war with Philippe. We can have no ugly squabbles at Versailles; they must see us live in harmony. You will curb your pride, and be a dutiful wife. Agreed?

Henriette (*swallows hard*) Agreed.

Louis Colbert! (*He beckons Colbert to them.*) Return to the city. Inform the tribunal I'll address them tomorrow.

Colbert Yes, Majesty.

Louise coughs. Louis notices and beckons her over to them. Henriette goes discreetly to Philippe.

Louis Before you go, Colbert, there is to be another new arrival. (*He touches Louise's belly.*) Do you think your charming wife might be able to . . .?

Colbert I am sure we can take this one as well, Majesty.

Louise Thank you so much, Monsieur. I know you will bring them up expertly.

Louis Leave us.

   Colbert bows and exits.

Now, on to the hothouse! La Quintinie has an asparagus!

Philippe At this time of year . . .!

Louis Oh, La Quintinie is a genius. He's grown six kinds of strawberries, and seven kinds of melons. He has lettuce in March, and peas in May! And a wonderful new fruit from Cyprus.

Henriette What's that?

Louis Called a 'cauliflower'. Entirely delicious!

Henriette (*takes Philippe's hand*) Let's go and see it, Philippe.

   Philippe is considerably surprised, but rather pleasantly so. He and Henriette exit. Louise follows them. Anne hangs back.

Louis (*to himself*) And all *he* could manage was an apricot. – Mother, what is the matter?

Anne This immorality nauseates me. The Queen is confined with yet another child, whilst you walk freely with your mistress. Grandees are turned into servants, and clerks are your confidential friends! Not one member of any aristocratic family has a post! Not a duke! Not even a chevalier!

Louis Yes, and we are safe in our beds.

Anne The world is mad. You are no king! Your mind is stuck on gardening, and fostering your bastards, and paying Molière good money to insult us! And why does everyone have to live here, in filthy Versailles?

Louis So I can keep an eye on them, Mother. Philippe's new code of conduct keeps them under my control. Those I distrust, I appoint to offices demanding daily attendance on my person. Former warlords now assist me when I sit on my commode. Conspirators have to hand me my stockings. Great princes, once ferocious, row the ladies on the lake . . .! I am thinking I am starting to have order here at last. – Now, let's go and inspect these vegetables. Cauliflower! What do you think of that?

Louis gives Anne his arm and they exit.

SCENE NINETEEN

A dungeon in the fortress of Pinerolo. Fouquet emerges from a corner. His fine clothes are filthy and torn. He's been there for some time.

Fouquet Some say power's an illusion. But Louis is the master of illusion. He has turned government into a spectacle, politics into a circus. The state as theatre, his life the drama. And the curtains are opened and closed by my old friend Jean-Baptiste, the forger of falsehoods, the fabricator of facts, who is all the while lining his pockets. You'd think there'd be turmoil, you'd think there'd be plotting and schism. But there is none. It's peaceful and quiet. The plucking of capons, uncorking of bottles, the family talking at table. (*Pause.*) Banished! I was looking forward to the West Indies for a few minutes but then the King rode up and overturned the verdict: imprisonment –

for life! So they put me here, in Pinerolo. Deep in the Alps of Savoy. (*Pause.*) I think sometimes of writing my memoirs, but they will not allow me a pen. Anyway what would it add up to? A tale of vanity and shipwreck. Hardly worth the ink. A dance of self-importance as the tide of death comes in . . . little prick flapping in the wind . . . Are not all fallen men pathetic? (*angrily*) He stole everything from me! I was wreathed in triumph, emblazoned in praise, the sun shining out of my arsehole. I loved my elegant château, the graceful arabesques of my parterres, my sheets and falls of water. I took such trouble to acquire it! Now I'll never see it again. (*He weeps.*) I'll never see my orange trees . . . (*He pulls himself together.*) What drives us to do this to ourselves? What vanity fires the ovens of our over-cooked ambition? Knowing it can end in Pinerolo? – declaiming, in the dark of a dungeon, the risible rhetoric of ruin. Is it pride? I was proud. But I was made a sacrifice, if not exactly virginal, to the boy they are calling the Sun King.

Slow fade.

The End.